HOW I BUILT A LOG CABIN IN THE WOODS

A TRUE STORY

DAN FIELDS

ISBN 978-0-9990986-3-9

DEDICATION

This book of two true stories is dedicated to you, the reader because of your avid interest in reading exciting and true stories. These stories follow two important adventures in my life and how I faced unusual challenges. So, open this book and your mind, and discover and learn. Settle back now in a comfortable chair, relax, and enjoy the read, because you deserve the best.

To: Pat
my Very Best
Wishes. Dan Fields

CONTENTS
Table of Contents

ACKNOWLEDGMENTS

First and foremost, I should like to thank my daughter, Dr. Brooke Jones, for her undying effort and expertise of book publishing in getting this book into a printed form. Without her patience, and knowledge of writing, this book would not have been published. Daughters are the best.

I would like to acknowledge my Mom and Dad for providing me with the first inkling that I would like to have a log cabin. It was during the Great Depression when jobs were scarce, and to be employed, one had to travel to where the jobs were. It was during this "travel period" that my parents rented a two-room log house at the edge of a dense forest for fifty cents per month. My Dad was away most of the time leaving me there with my Mom, older brother Joe, and younger brother Don. The front porch was situated on the east side of the cabin where in the summer evenings my mother and I would sit out there, and between the calls of the Whippoorwills and the blinking lights of the fire-flies, she told me countless stories of how things came to be. We had many good times in that simple dwelling, and those good feelings became associated with being in a log house and I was determined to build me a log cabin and restore those good feelings.

Last but not least, I would like to acknowledge that the time I spent hiking and camping out in the rugged mountains of Colorado with the late, Lee Minton, was most educational. He took me to many abandoned, but completely furnished, log cabins, where I acquired the necessary knowledge of how a log cabin was constructed and the enthusiasm to get one of my own built. Thank you, Lee.

HOW I BUILT A LOG CABIN
IN THE WOODS
WITH SIMPLE HAND TOOLS

A TRUE STORY

DAN FIELDS

HOW I BUILT A LOG CABIN IN THE WOODS

A true story

I'm not telling you How To Build a Cabin,
I am only sharing How I Built My Cabin.

"My most important tip
to anyone building a cabin
in the woods, is to cut the logs
above your cabin site."

Alternative Title
A ROOF IMPERVIOUS TO RAIN

A lifetime dream of mine was to have a log cabin in the woods of my own and built by my own hands. Having this dream to hang on to got me through some very rough times. This dream was instilled in my mind a long time ago when I was very young. I lived in such a dwelling with my mother, father, and two brothers. It had only two rooms, no electricity, no telephone, no running water, (except in the stream that was located nearby.), but all those were negatives based upon today's standards and was not at all that bad to live with at that time. On the positive side of my story and imbedded in my memory was the front porch situated on the east side of the cabin where in the summer evenings my mother and I would sit out there, and between the calls of the Whippoorwills and the blinking lights of the fire-flies, she told me countless stories of how things came to be.

The school bus dropped me off on the road about a mile from the house and after walking down the lane through the woods to the log house it was always a joyful welcome to come inside and be greeted by the soothing aroma of freshly baked bread and the warmth of the wood stove.

Memories like those were the catalysts that kept my dream alive and eventually I reached the time in my life where I was able to make it come true. And so, it was that I commenced.

The contents of this writing are not intended as an instruction manual or a how to do it book. No, not in the least. What it is though is just a story, a true one at that, of how I built a log cabin in the woods high up in the Rocky Mountains. So now my story begins.

Part One

My wife shared my dream of a place in the woods and that of course was a real plus when the actual construction took me away and left her alone. She too looked forward to the day that it was completed so her support was one hundred percent.

I stated that she shared my interests in that regard and to that end she and I, prior to any start, would spend the weekends hiking around high up in the Rockies looking for just the right place.

We did not find it right away, as that would have been too much of a dream come true. It took a lot of work and a lot of bivouacking around the hills, sleeping out under the stars and a lot of putting up with the elements. I do not know how many cans of pork & beans and wieners we consumed on these treks. On many occasions during our search we found numerous abandoned cabins throughout the woods that afforded us a place of refuge and a headquarters to leave our sleeping bags and groceries.

I had certain requirements that must be met for the place I wanted for the cabin site. Many attractive locations I dismissed because one or more of the requirements were missing. I will enumerate them now and they are as follows:

1. <u>South side of the mountain</u>. I wanted my cabin to rest on the south side of the slope as that affords sunshine for the most of the time and when it did snow it would not last as long and would not last as long on the ground when spring approached. It might be summed up as <u>a southern exposure.</u>

2. <u>Pine Trees.</u> It would be most difficult to build a log cabin without an abundance of pine trees with which to construct it.

3. <u>Water.</u> I did not want the laborious task of having to lug water for all of my needs. So, my location must have a source of water.

One way or another. Pond, creek, spring, river, or lake.

4. <u>A Road.</u>   Roads are a very useful element. It does not have to be the best in the west, but even the worst road beats having to head out with a Jeep full of stuff dodging trees, stumps, rocks and whatever. I might add that the one I wound up with was little more than a dried-up creek bed, but that afforded me adequate ingress and egress.

As stated in my first requirement, I wanted a spot on the sunny side of the slope, but to find it I first spent a lot of time on the north side of a slope looking across at it through binoculars. It's interesting how much ground you can cover with that method.   The best place for that method was a large mine dump, or tailings, high above the treetops, afforded me a good look across the valley. Also, at the other end of the tailings was a very old and dilapidated miner's cabin who's only saving grace was its tin roof and its four walls. But these attributes did provide my wife and me with somewhat comfortable headquarters.

Anyway, when looking through the binoculars, I learned that at certain times of the day a road, a tailings dump, or a clearing could not be discerned. So, on a warm summer day, I had to go over the area both in the morning hours and then again in the afternoon hours.

So, late in the afternoon I was sitting on the edge of some ancient tailings training my binoculars at the mountain across the valley. The sun was just right and its light revealed a road and visually I slowly followed its course as it switch-backed its way up the side of the mountain. In places trees or large boulders obscured it, but I was able to trace it up to a point where a gulch ran alongside it.

Seeing the gulch was encouraging to me in that it implied a mountain stream might be found flowing within its banks. Then the road turned to the right and was lost from view in a thick forest of tall pines. My heart skipped a beat as I pondered if that could be the right place.

I again scanned the road and this time I focused my attention on locating some outstanding landmarks. There was a large boulder with a small pine tree on its top and that boulder rested about a distance of a block, I guessed, from a sharp left turn in the road. On up from the boulder the road ran straight and then veered to the right for a straight stretch to my selected spot and then it turned sharply to the right disappearing into the trees.

I made a rough sketch of the road on a piece of paper indicating where the boulder might be from the curve, stowed it in my jacket pocket, cased up the binoculars and then went in to the cabin where my wife had supper ready. Over the meal, I revealed to her what I had found. We both agreed that in the morning, after breaking camp, we'd head out down the mountain and up the other side to locate that road.

Before we left that morning, there was one thing I wanted to do before leaving. Since the spot, I had located seemed to be about level with where I stood I thought it might be a good idea to erect some sort of marker here that could be seen from that spot. It would serve as a bearing in case I got confused, which is easily done when one gets into a bunch of trees. I found an old and rusty one-inch pipe about eight feet in length, tied one of my old T-shirts[1] to it and hoisted it aloft held in place with some boards and rocks.

---

[1] All of my T-shirts were old.

Eureka

There was a very rough looking road leading up into the direction we wanted to go, and close to the mouth of this road stood a two-room cabin occupied by an Old Timer who agreed to let us park in front of his place.

Our vehicle was a 1946 CJ-2A military Jeep and in it we had negotiated quite a few rough roads. However, this road, with its abundance of jagged rocks and high centering deep ruts did not look too promising to drive up. We might get way up into it with no place to turn around and have to navigate backwards all the way back down, and I am the world's worst Jeep backer upper. So, on this bright and sunny early August morning we opted to park the Jeep and head out up the road on foot.

We found, however, that the worst part of the road was the beginning, and some places were downright a decent road. Two places though of concern were slanted so badly from dirt washing down that a Jeep could easily turn over, so after coming to these I was glad that we had decided to go on foot.

After considerable climbing, we arrived at the curve that turned to the left. There we stopped to rest and while doing so I got out the binoculars and scanned the opposite side of the mountain trying to locate my T-shirt on the pole, but could not find it. The curve, however, was very washed out and to get a Jeep around it would take considerable amount of filling in.

Continuing on then up the road a short way from the curve we came upon a large boulder on our right sitting at the edge of the road. I climbed around it to its top looking for the tree that I thought was on it, but there was none. What I had seen through the binoculars was a tree growing behind the rock, but from where I had been looking it appeared to be growing out of the top of the boulder. I got out the binoculars and focused them across to the other mountain. I had to shade them from the sun, but then I discerned a white object above the tailings. It was my T-shirt. This then was the boulder I had seen yesterday and we were on the right road.

About a half mile on up from the boulder the road veered slightly to the right and the gulch was quite evident now. I was curious to see if any water was flowing in it so I left my wife on the road and hiked down to the bottom. She welcomed the rest as we had hiked quite a distance and all up hill.

Getting down to the bottom of the gulch I found a nice steady stream of cool fresh water. That was a good showing as most small streams are long gone by August. I was thirsty any way so I gave it a good test. It was cool, sweet, and very soft. I then scurried back up the slope to tell my wife of the good news.

Returning back up to the road I had to rest several times as the slope up from the stream was very steep and I was tired out anyway from the hike up the road. So, I rested a bit longer at this point.

During this rest, I reviewed the notes I had taken yesterday. The road should run on a straight course for a distance and then turn sharply to the right.

We continued on upward and at this point the road became steeper and for a couple of tired hikers it was rough going, but it would be very passable by a Jeep not having any rocks or ruts to navigate. Soon we arrived at the curve and noticed that the gulch ended abruptly giving way to a steep rise covered with an abundance of buck brush, rocks, and Junipers. We went off the road to the left negotiating a slight slope to the rim of the gulch and peered down. The water was still there but ended at the base of the steep rise. We made our way down the bank to the water's edge and discovered that it originated from out of the rise. It was a spring and flowing quite steadily. We took a long drink from it and then made our way back up to the top. Straight and tall White Pines were in abundance along with a fine stand of Lodge Pole Pine, Pole Pine, and right then we decided that, as Brigham Young once said, this is the Place.

It had a road, (such as it was) a stream, on the south side, and lots of trees.

Illustrations from the iournal of Dan Fields ©1980

I located the spot on my topography map as being in section 31, and several days later I was in the office of the USGS. I was there requesting a Photostat copy of the plat for that section. The plat was full of claims, each one totaled 5 acres or so, and in the center of each one was the survey number. I found the one showing the stream and road (it was referred to as a wagon road on the plat), but cutting across it was another one overlapping it by a little bit, in fact the plat showed numerous claims that

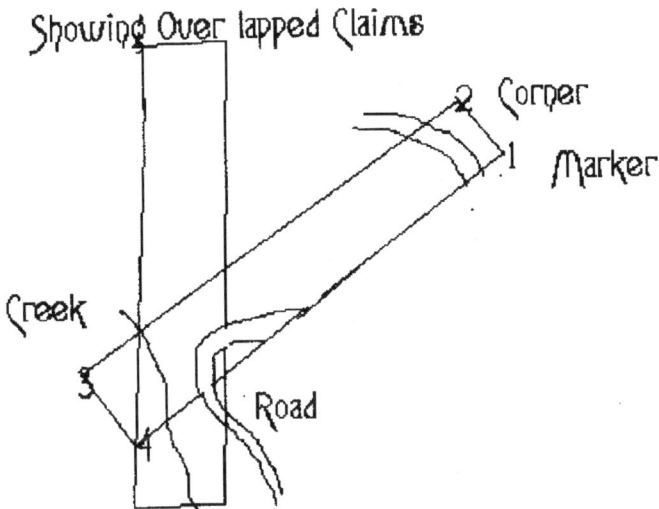

Illustrations from the journal of Dan Fields ©1980

overlapped the other and it made me wonder how the miners could prove on whose claim a mineral strike was made.

The two overlapped claims resembled an x that is taller at the top than at the bottom. The attendant said that those were in *conflict* and both should be considered as one. I then requested the field notes of those two survey numbers.

The attendant handed me a very old book with pages in vintage script. I was not allowed to take it out of the office so I copied the notes on paper and I might add it took me nearly all day to do that. Also, I learned that the *footage* is listed in the left-hand margin and I was told to copy it that way so when it's done the total footage can be easily ascertained.

The next Saturday we returned to the place armed not only with the field notes, but our sleeping bags and two days' supply of food, a compass we had found in a box of cracker jacks, and a fifty-foot length of clothes line rope. Not quite the surveyors complement, but adequate for our needs.

By the time we reached the spot, we were quite worn out for as I've stated, the road is quite steep and we were carrying a lot of stuff. After resting for a while we decided it best to make a shelter for the night and not do any surveying.

Locating a dug-out area that was reasonably level, I drug up a half dozen or so of downed

Illustrations from the journal of Dan Fields ©1980

aspens and made a lean-to then covered it with a plastic sheet. She scoured around gathering up firewood for the evening meal and for the night, I cleared a wide area and built a fire ring and placed a metal grate across it. In no time at all we were ready for the night.

After supper was over we meandered up the road a way to another curve that went to the left. This curve was also shown on the plat and mentioned in the field notes, but we were too tired to do any more looking around. We returned and hit the sack and our tired bones overcame our anxiety. The gentle wind in the trees and the sounds of the night faded away and before we knew it, morning had arrived.

We finished breakfast and while sipping a hot cup of coffee, we went over the field notes and plat again. Some of the markers were shown to be on the other side of the stream, but it was so steep in that direction that we decided it would be easier to look for the markers just off the upper curve. According to the notes, if we followed the road to the upper curve, corner number twelve could be found about ten feet just off the road.

We headed out in that direction taking with us the compass, field notes, and the clothes line rope. Arriving at the curve we stopped and studied that portion of the notes with earnest. It stated that a stone around two feet high had the number 12 and the survey number chiseled on it. And then up higher on the hill one hundred feet from that stone was another stone with the number 11 and the survey number chiseled on it.

Looking at the notes early on it seemed simple to just walk off the road about ten feet and there would be the stone. But here at the curve we faced a bank so steep we had to walk way around it to our right and then try and find our way back. Well that wasn't so easy. Returning to where we thought the curve was, it was blocked from our view by a heavy and thick stand of gooseberry bushes. Neither could we see any portion of the road. And to make it worse, the stone had been put in place around 1890 and might be covered by a bunch of duff gathering density for all those years.

We wrestled our way around much of the brush looking at stumps that resembled large stones and inspected, I don't know how many large stones. Since we couldn't see the road or the curve our bearings soon became lost. But we continued on. Suddenly my wife called out. "I found it."

With much excitement, I rushed over. She was busily brushing off the debris to make the markings more legible. Then she read the inscription and exclaimed, "Eleven. This is marker number eleven." We had wandered that far off. But we were elated. At last we had identified the property. Well, at least one corner of it.

We knew then that the marker number 12

was one hundred feet back down, so we stretched out the clothes line rope for fifty feet, took a bearing on the compass. We stretched it out again. She poked a stick in the ground where it ended, but there was not a large stone where it ended. We looked about the area. Then we saw a hump of duff about five feet to the right. We scraped it all away revealing a stone with a 12 chiseled near its top. We had found it.

Having gained the experience of finding markers now we set out to locate the rest of them and with luck, we found them.

Our next move now was to go to the courthouse at the county seat and check the tax rolls. We figured that this piece of property had held someone's interest away back then only for the minerals it might give up, and with that played out, so did the interest, and it had gone back to the county for taxes.

Our visit to the courthouse proved us

correct. There were back taxes due in an amount, fortunately, that we could afford. We purchased the property on the spot. It did have to be advertised for a few times to give the previous owner a chance to redeem it, but no one came forth so late in October the land became ours.

I knew I couldn't do any construction because winter was fast approaching, but I figured if I cut down the trees now, hopefully they would be dry enough to build with come next May. It had snowed now a few times, but none of it lasted very long on the ground. Just in the shady spots.

Now I needed to know just how many trees had to be felled to build the cabin. With a pencil, paper and my best mathematical ability and several sketches later, I came up with the figure of forty-four which I arrived at this way. I would select the trees with at least an eight-inch butt and a seven or six-inch top (which would be more of a guess as its hard to judge twenty feet up). Then as I laid each log in place I would try and maintain a distance of ten inches from the top of the bottom log to the top of the log above it. Chinking would fill in the open space between them. Eleven logs then on each four sides would reach the height of one hundred inches, which would be just a little higher than eight feet. That height would be more than enough height to accommodate a standard size door and headroom. I could easily maintain the ten-inch standard by adjusting the depth of the corner notching.

It will require a little more than forty-four when you figure the purlins (I planned to use Lodge Pole Pines for these), and whatever else I planned to make with logs.

I decided to cut the trees out of the stand near the upper curve, as I knew exactly where the markers were, which would keep me out of the National Forest. Also, getting the logs to the cabin site from the upper curve would be easier as it was all downhill.

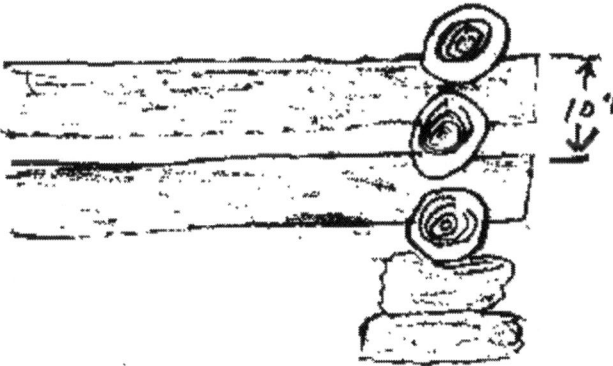

Illustrations from the journal of Dan Fields ©1980

I purchased a cross cut saw from Wards (I could not afford a chain saw), about three and half feet long with deep-set teeth. And, fortunately for me, a friend, Roy, had just purchased a new ax and wanted to try it out, so

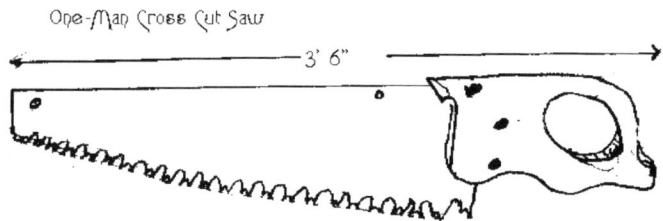

One-Man Cross Cut Saw

3' 6"

Illustrations from the journal of Dan Fields ©1980

he volunteered to come up and notch (cut a wedge) in the trees for the direction for them to fall.

That really helped me immensely not only in cutting the notch, but he was very good at selecting the straightest trees at the right diameter. While he was doing, that I was sawing away. The project went well as the sap was down into the roots making the ax and saw bites an easier task.

Roy had to leave after he had notched all of the trees so I was left alone to finish felling the trees. I finished the project about an hour before dark and quit in time to fix supper while there was enough light. I curled up in my sleeping bag under the lean-to and fell right to sleep.

I was awakened early the next morning by the cackling of two Magpies fussing over some trivial tidbit of food and then I realized it wasn't such a trivial tidbit at all. They had somehow gotten into my loaf of bread, so I jumped out of the sleeping bag and shooed them off. I was able to salvage most of it.

I had a laborious enterprise ahead of me so

I figured I needed a most wholesome breakfast consisting of a big can of Pork & Beans. And that enterprise for the day was to remove all limbs and branches and to saw off the tops of each tree.

Yesterday I had left the big saw up there under a clump of rabbit brush so I only carried a small hatchet and a small bucksaw. There were not that many limbs to trim off and sawing the tops off went much faster than it did to cut the tree down as the top was smaller in diameter than the trunk. Also, it was easier in that the tree was down so I could saw in a much better and less tiring position.

I had decided that the size of the cabin would be fifteen by twenty feet inside. So, to allow a foot overhang on each corner, I cut off the tops of 22 logs at seventeen-feet, and the remainder at twenty-two feet.

I completed the whole task by noon. I was

very proud of myself, and elated that this part of the project was finished. I did not dwell on the fact that I had just started and I had a long way to go and much effort lay before me.

I returned to my camp with my tools, sat down and munched on a peanut butter and jelly sandwich. And while eating, I pondered my next move. One thing for sure, I did not relish having to walk up to here so I decided my next project should be the improvement of the road making it possible to get the Jeep through.

Also, I wanted to drag the logs down to the site and would definitely need the Jeep for that. So, as I continued eating I mulled over in my mind the tools needed and when to get on to it.

One determining factor was the good weather, and I chose to take advantage of that.

It was still early in the day, and I had the pick and shovel in the Jeep below, so I decided to go with it. I hiked down the road to commence my new project.

I could not drive the Jeep too far up at the mouth of the road because of the large rocks and the ruts, so I had to tackle that obstacle first. To my surprise the large rocks were loose and I easily pried them out of the way with the shovel (or spade), and the ruts I filled with smaller rocks. It wasn't the best repair resulting in the best of roads, but now the Jeep would not hit high center.

I shifted into four-wheel drive, low range, and slowly drove the Jeep up over my repaired area and continued on until I reached the first *slant*. This *slant* ran for about only ten feet, but it would be enough to cause a major tip over and there was no way around it. The left side of the road was edged by a bank that rose nearly straight up, and on the right side was a sheer straight drop-off with no trees or boulders that afforded a stop to a Jeep rolling down it.

My plan was to pick ax the high side and deposit the dirt into the low side, that made sense, but the ground was so hard packed that it proved too laborious and I tired too quickly. This would not do the trick. Then I tested the dirt on the bank and it was much looser and could be moved without having to pick it out.

But first I placed a row of rocks at the edge of the low side as a support and commenced filling in the area with the dirt. It filled quickly to where I had to add another row of rocks. In less than an hour I had raised the low side

Illustrations from the journal of Dan Fields ©1980

around a foot, high enough to cross over safely.

The next *slant* was not nearly as long or slanted as the first one, but still posed a hazard. Since I had experience on this type of repair, I accomplished it in a very short time.

As to the curve on ahead with its washed-out condition, it was wide enough to go around it. I cringed a little bit going around it because I had to keep the right wheels a little way up the bank causing the Jeep to lean precariously. I did manage to get around it, but then I stopped, realizing that I would have to come back this way. It would be more difficult to negotiate the curve with gravity pulling me downward. So, I got out and studied it for a moment. The washed-out area was too deep for just shoveling dirt into it, so I filled it up with a bunch of rocks, which I rolled down from above. Always move rocks by rolling them downhill. It's much easier that way.

It didn't take too long to fill up the ditch and I felt better knowing I wouldn't have any trouble on the way down.

The remainder of the trip up to the cabin site was, as they say. "A piece of cake."

I turned off to the left into my campsite and parked the Jeep a little way off the road. I realized that the slope was rather slanted. Not enough to tip the Jeep over, but it would be too difficult to do any type of constructing and it would be nice to have a level spot. Often time's things appear different when traversed on foot.

But I dismissed that problem for a moment because I hadn't yet given any thought as to the exact spot to erect the cabin. That was my next assignment, and before dark I had it all worked out.

"I looked all over and found

the right place,

Midst the pines and Aspens

where my cabin would grace."

The only logical place was between the road and the stream. That was easy. Studying every aspect and lay of the land, I concluded that the best place to build it was where I had my lean-to. It was a natural depression, nearly the right dimensions, and just a little bit of excavation would accommodate the size cabin I was planning. Some of the south side would need a rock wall, but not that much to create a real hassle. The bottom log on the south side would run twenty feet across the depression. The first five feet of the log would be nearly at ground level and so would the last five feet, requiring ten feet in the center of the log and roughly three feet down to wall up. But since the depression tapered downward on the left side and then up on the right side it would not be all ten feet across and three feet down. And in the center of the wall would be a handy place to build a door for storing things underneath.

I turned in that night with the vision that on this very spot where I was lying would someday soon have a fine and well-built cabin, or at least a cabin.

A slight breeze came up and created a relaxing night song as it tiptoed its way among the boughs of the tall pines. It brought with it the first taste of the approaching winter, but my sleeping bag was warm and I pulled the edges closer to my face. I must get those logs down here tomorrow.

The wind played with the embers of my campfire and their popping and snapping soon faded from my conscious mind as I fell off to sleep, tired but contented with the accomplishments of the day.

The Driveway

I not only needed a level place to park the Jeep, but I also wanted a level place to store the logs on for the winter. So, it was logical to assume that the driveway should be my next assignment.

I did not know how much time this project would require, but if all failed and winter came suddenly upon me; the logs would still be there next May. The month of May was just a month I had surmised that I could get back up here, and it proved out to be right.

I measured three feet on either side of the Jeep and staked it out. That width of a driveway would allow a driver and a passenger to alight from the Jeep with no trouble. Then I backed the Jeep out into the road.

In line with the downhill stakes, I placed rocks in a row to the edge of the road. My plan was the same as I had applied when I worked on the *slants* by picking the dirt loose on the high side and shovels it into the low side against the rocks.

The dirt, mostly gravel, was soft from the melted snow and was easy to pick and to shovel. The amount filled up the row of rocks, and soon I had to add another row, and then another one. Thankfully, being in the Rockies there is no problem of finding rocks. The task was moving along faster than I could have hoped for.

I stopped a few times to rest and to grab a snack, but did not want to stop too long as I wanted this job done so I could get on with the cabin building. Here to for, all the work I had done was not getting the actual construction started, and now I was more anxious than ever. So that anxiety added impetus to the effort at hand and I worked at it with much vigor.

As I picked away at the topside I would uncover rocks, which I placed on the row of rocks, which saved me from having to search around for them. The time passed quickly and the low side grew taller.

The row of rocks now took on the appearance of a retaining wall and the once tall side was now a dirt bank of nearly three feet high. The length of the driveway, to my estimation, ran about 25 feet from the road to the rise of the bluff that sloped down to the stream.

It was about five thirty when I decided the driveway was sufficiently done. I stopped my shoveling, and then went down to the stream and washed up.

I got a fire going and opened up a can of beef

stew, and cooked it in the can. I built just a small fire and placed the can of stew in it with the lid still intact to prevent stuff getting into it. Using small twigs, I stood them upright around the can, teepee style, and as they burned away I would replace them with more. This method heated the can all the way around thus eliminating the need for a roaring fire.

Illustrations from the journal of Dan Fields ©1980

I awoke the next morning to another dusting of snow indicative that winter was definitely on its way. But it didn't last on the ground too long and didn't impede my progress that I was to make that day. And that was to get the logs down from where they lay and stack them above the cabin site.

I figured by having them above the site I would have a downhill advantage when the time came to start the construction. My plan was to drag the logs down to the curve, then haul them up the bank and stack them just above the proposed site. I backed the Jeep out to the road and decided to drive up the bank without the weight of pulling a log. Finding a place that appeared less steep, I attempted to drive up it, but to no avail. Nothing accomplished but two deep ruts where the tires had dug in. The bank was too steep and the dirt too loose. I would not be able to get any logs up behind the site. I thought it over and made up my mind to drag the logs down and stack them in the driveway, and come next May I'd have to use some device to help get the logs from the driveway up to the site a distance of 10 to 15 feet.

I then drove up to where the logs lay. Since the bank up there was also steep I could not get real close to the logs. I left the Jeep parked in the road. With a long and strong rope from my block and tackle, I snaked the logs out to the road one at a time, piling them up. I figured that having a downhill advantage I could easily drag three at once. And I had snaked three out, I hooked them onto the Jeep. At this time, I thought that was a good idea as if I got them all out on the road at once, and if anybody happened to come along, I would have the road blocked.

I spent all of that day dragging the 44 logs down to the driveway. They took up most of the driveway, especially in length, but it was wide enough to still accommodate the Jeep.

I still needed four more logs for purlins, which I planned to take from the stand of Lodge Pole Pines. These would be much smaller in diameter, around four inches, and I wanted to get those cut and stacked with the rest so they too would be dry enough come next May.

As tired as I was I decided to go ahead and get that done while the weather was good. Up here at this altitude one can never guess what's in store for tomorrow.

So, I drove the Jeep to the upper curve armed with a hatchet and my big saw. All the Lodge Poles were straight as an arrow and finding just four was no problem. I felled the four without too much effort, cut the tops out at seventeen feet, and had hardly any limbs to trim off.

They were much lighter than the big ones and I was able to drag all of them at once down to the driveway.

I was cold and hungry and in need of a hot cup of coffee. For that I would need a bigger fire, but since the wind was a little severe I gathered several more rocks to make my fire ring higher. I was always concerned with forest fires.

Looking in my supply of grub I found a can of pork & beans, a can of Boyardee, a pack of crackers, a small can of coffee grounds, and a pack of Swisher Sweet cigars. I went to the stream and filled up my small teakettle, came back, got the fire going, opened both cans and set them and the teakettle in the fire. I wouldn't have anything left for breakfast, but that was tomorrow, and I'm hungry now. I dumped the coffee grounds into the teakettle and soon it was boiling.

The meal over, I settled back in the seat with a hot steaming cup of coffee and the soothing aroma of a fine cigar, and looking up at the star-studded sky, I thought to myself. Life couldn't be any better than this.

———⟫⟨———

Part Two

The winter months in Denver seemed extremely long, as I was anxious to get started on building the cabin. I knew though that even if it wasn't winter I shouldn't be doing any construction as the logs should season and dry out good. So, it was some consolation that when May arrived the logs would be ready.

I took this opportunity trying to collect my thoughts, but did a lot of day dreaming about the cabin. Floorboards; spikes; nails; roofing; tarpaper, and insulation were constantly on my mind. Then I got serious and began jotting down on paper some calculations of what materials I would require and how much of it.

For the flooring and the roof, I wavered between using eight-inch wide boards or sheets of plywood. The sheets of plywood had an advantage in that when laid would cover a lot more space than a single board. And in thinking of it covering more space I had to considering how much space it would require on the Jeep.

A 1" x 8" x 8' board would be much easier to lift and move up and down than a sheet of plywood. In getting them up the steep road on the small Jeep, I figured by putting the windshield down and removing the passenger seat I could easily carry about twenty boards much easier than I could sheets of plywood.

So, the decision was made then to use boards for the flooring and the roofing.

Floor Boards

My calculations showed that 46 boards were needed to cover the 15' x 20' flooring detailed as follows:

23 - 1" x 8" x 12', and 23- 1" x 8" x 8'.

The cabin width being 15 feet equals 180 inches, and using 8-inch wide boards, so dividing 180 by 8 would total 22.5 rows of boards (I rounded it up to 23).

The boards would run staggered the 20 feet, i.e. one row would be a 12-foot board and an 8-foot board. The next row would be an 8-foot board and a 12-foot board. This method would help to prevent a sagging in the floor.

Roof Boards

The Number of Roof Boards Required is as Follows:

30 - 1" x 8" x 12' and 30 - 1" x 8"x 10'

Figuring out how many boards were needed for the roof was basically the same as that of the floor except that it would require more boards. I calculated their number as follows:

I determined that the pitch (or ridge height) of the roof would be one-third the width of the cabin. So, the cabin being fifteen feet wide, the pitch then would be five feet high. (I don't know if I learned this from somewhere or if I just made it up.) So, saying the height of 5 feet is A, one half of the cabin width of 7.5 feet is B, by using the Pythagorean theorem of $A^2+B^2 = C^2$, or A is 25 B is 56.25. The sum of these two equals 81.25. Figuring the square root then of 81.25

would be a little over 9, and to make it easier and allowing for an overhang, I increased it to 10. So, the slant of the roof would run 10 feet from the ridge to the overhang.

Now to calculate the number of boards needed:

Ten feet equals 120 inches. Dividing that by 8 inches gives me 15 rows of boards. Allowing for an overhang of a foot, I figured the row should equal twenty-two feet.

Each row would consist of 1 twelve-foot long board and 1 ten-foot long board, and stagger them like I planned to do with the floorboards.

So, then the total of the roof boards would be 15 - 1"x 8"x 12', and 15 - 1" x 8" x 10', and double each amount to accommodate the other side of the roof, or 30 twelve footers, and 30 ten footers, for a total of 60 boards.

I want to digress from this configuration for a while to mention what luck I started having. I'll get back to the rest of the materials later on, but first I want to mention that I had driven up to the mountains early in January and of course the snow was too deep to go anywhere. So, I stopped off at the cabin of the 'Old Timer'. As we were having coffee the subject of the building materials came up and I happened to mention that my neighbors would not appreciate my piling all of them up in my yard. It was then that he said he had a clear spot down below his cabin and I could pile them there. "It would keep people from parking there," he said. "You could bring them up a little bit at a time."

I thanked him for the coffee and the offer of his clear spot. I did not realize at the time how important that was going to be.

Another significant bit of luck came my way when I learned that a contractor had received a notice from the city to mow down the weeds in his vacant lot. But it was full of planks and not wanting to haul them away to the dump, he was offering them to anyone who came by. Well, it goes without saying, I jumped at the chance and I was at his vacant lot the next morning with a U-Haul trailer. The contractor met me there saying he would appreciate my taking them all away so he could mow the field in time to save having to pay a fine. He told me his name and it was a very unusual name, so unusual that when he left I wrote it down and I was glad I did as that helped me later on.

I can't tell you how elated I was when I saw the number of planks in that lot. There were numerous two by fours, two by sixes, and two by eights, ranging in various lengths from 8 feet to 12 feet. I immediately got busy sorting the planks into sizes and then loaded them onto the trailer according to their size.

I knew the Jeep could not pull such a load so I had to make two trips. It took all of that day to clear out the lot, but with the first and second load I drove straight up to the "Old Timer's" place and unloaded them.

I wrote down the best I could the number of each different size and on returning home I figured that I had acquired more than enough material for the rafters and the floor joists.

Now, all I had to concentrate on was the boards for the roof and the floor. And they came shortly after that windfall.

I read an advertisement in a Saturday's paper that a certain lumber company had a bad fire in its building and yard, and was having a fire sale the next day, Sunday.

I felt this might be an opportunity to acquire my lumber at a much lower price. So, I rented the U-Haul trailer that afternoon and was at the lumberyard early the next morning. The sale was just getting started.

I asked the first fellow I met, who worked there, about the prices of my needed boards and he said that I'd have to speak with the one in charge of the sale. Then he motioned with his hand toward a fellow in a red shirt, the one with his back to me.

I walked over to him, he was speaking with someone else, so I waited until he was finished, and then I spoke. He turned around. I recognized him right off as the contractor, Mr. So, and So with the odd name. After the greetings were over I told him what I needed. He said, "He so appreciated my clearing out his vacant lot, and also that I had remembered his name, which no one ever could." As a result, he said, "I could have all of the boards I wanted for a nickel a foot."

The trailer was wide enough to lay 10 boards

in each row so I stacked up ten rows which was a total of 110 boards, six more than I needed, at a cost of only $55, and I purchased a roll of plastic sheeting. I left there straight for the "Old Timers" house and after dropping off the boards; I covered them and the planks with the plastic.

On the way to returning the trailer, I really felt good as though a major hurtles had been overcome. But now May seemed much further away and I wished it was here already, but I then recalled what my Mother always said when I made a wish like that. "You're wishing your life away." So, I quit wishing and accepted the fact that May was three months away.

During those remaining winter months, I completed my configurations on materials I still needed. And then one day a fellow worker said he had just finished remolding his house and had some windows he'd like to get rid of and asked if I could use them. Strangely enough with all of my planning I hadn't thought about the windows. I readily accepted his offer. They were actually French Doors, but I was eager to get them and they worked out nicely.

I also found a good price on 8 inches and 12-inch spikes for a dime apiece. I planned to spike down the corners with the 8-inch and use the 12-inch for the centers.

Later on, as the construction began I would buy the stuff, as it was needed, such as nails, insulation, cement, roofing, etc.

<hr>

Part Three

Finally, May Arrived

The first week of May arrived. I had taken 3 weeks off from work and I headed for the hills. The Jeep was packed with plenty of grub, a Coleman stove, pick ax, shovel, hatchet, chisel, saws, spikes, hammer, level, ball of string, 7 lb. sledge hammer with a short handle, a sack of 8d nails, a sack of 10 d nails, ice tongs, dividers (which were not too effective) and a box of chalk.

I stopped at the "Old Timer's" cabin first off. The plastic over the lumber had seen some rough weather, but had done its job well in defying the harsh elements.

The "Old Timer'" said he had hiked up there just yesterday to my place and that there were a couple of snow drifts I'd have to get over, but he assured me that they didn't appear to be too deep. But he did caution me not to try and haul any of the lumber up there not knowing for sure about the drifts.

"Have you got a pick and shovel?" he asked. "I'll loan you mine," he added. I said I did.

We had coffee together and made small talk, but I was anxious to get up there, so I refused a second cup of coffee. But he did give me an invitation to join him around six for supper, which I did accept. Then I was on my way.

I encountered the first snowdrift just past the boulder and hit it hard staying as far to the right as I could. I went right through it and also the other one, which lay about a block on up the road.

Reaching the site, I pulled off the road onto the driveway and parked in some patches of snow. None large enough to get the Jeep stuck. The logs had a little snow peeking through the cracks, but appeared dry.

I felt so elated. At last I could start the actual construction. A little snow was on the high end of the depression where my lean-to would sit, that had been shaded by a tall pine, but that would dry out all right.

<hr>

Now I had come to the point of the actual construction. This was to be the start and I must get it off right as anything done or placed wrong could have a dire affect all along the construction. So, I ran over in my mind exactly what should be done first and done right.

First, I had to lay out the dimensions of a cabin in the depression. The north and south side of the cabin would run 20 feet and the east and west side of the cabin would run 15 feet. I had brought a ball of string and stakes for this part, and not to mention, a 25-ft. tape measure. My rough stakeout showed that I had to do some excavation on the north side. I say rough because I was not at this time going to have each corner absolutely squared, as I needed to do some digging out.

I dug out the two corners on the north side, which proved to be easily done as the dirt was soft and did not require real deep digging. I measured it all again and this time tried to be a little more accurate.

I wanted two good-sized stones for each corner for the piers, and preferably with flat surfaces top and bottom. That took a little doing, but I managed to find them and I was smart enough to look for them above the cabin site.

Corner Stones or Piers

Illustrations from the journal of Dan Fields ©1980

I placed just one stone at a time in each corner. I was being serious now about squaring up each corner with the others. To get it accurate the stones would have to be shifted around probably several times, so I only wanted to have to move one stone. Once each corner is squared up I can place the second stone on top of the first stone. But of course, the real squaring up of the corners will come when I lay the first four logs.

My thought of placing two stones on each corner was that if moisture crept up because of capillary action, it would stop at the second stone. I don't know really if that is true, but I thought it was so that's why I used two stones.

"My God", I exclaimed out loud. "Would you believe it? I am ready to lay down the first log." I was so excited I nearly peed my pants.

I put on my heavy leather gloves and with the ice tongs, I took hold of the first 22-foot log. I tied a piece of rope between the two-ice tong handles so I could use it with one hand. The log was heavy but moveable. It was uphill all the way but the distance was only about 10 feet.

By lifting and/or dragging one end at a time I was able to "walk" it, slowly I might add, to the south side. I was going to place it on the corner stones of the south side, but changed my mind. Instead I lifted each end over those stones and continued walking the log on to the north corner stones. I reasoned that if I placed the first log on the south side I might knock it loose trying to get over it with the second log, as it would not be fastened down until the two logs running the 15 feet were in place. Before placing it on the pier I flattened out that part of the log that would rest on the stone, doing the same to the other end and also to the south log.

I placed one end carefully on top of the first set of corner stones, and then lifted the other end on top of the second set of corner stones.

The first log had been set in place. It didn't matter at this time which direction the ends faced, but it would from now on. Which I will explain:

I placed the north side log with the butt end facing the east.

I placed the south side log with the butt end facing the west.

I placed the west side log with the butt end facing the north and resting on the top end of the north side log, and its top end resting on the butt end of the south side log.

I placed the east side log with the butt end facing the south, resting on the top end of the south side log, and its top end resting on the butt end of the north side log.

Each corner then would consist of a butt end and a top end.

By five o' clock I had laid four logs making the first perimeter of the cabin. It had gone slow because of all the carefulness I had taken.

I notched each corner by using a small saw, a hatchet, and chisel, but I did not nail them in place just yet, as I might have to shift them around a little bit. I had to make absolutely sure that it was all-square and that the inside measurements were 15 feet and 20 feet. Once that was accomplished I could then nail down the corners.

One thing I will mention here, because I had no place to insert it above, is that when I finished notching the corners of the east and west log, I also cut a notch in each of their centers on the bottom. As you will read later, you will find out that the ends of a center log will fit into this notch. The center beam log runs parallel with the north and south logs and its purpose is to hold up the overlapped ends of the floor joists. Just thought I'd throw that in now. You'll learn how I fit it in later.

I squared each corner as I went using a builder's square, and with the tape measure I made sure that the correct inside length of 15 feet and 20 feet was maintained.

Soon, the corners were as square as I could get them what with the logs having rough and uneven sides.

Then I fastened each corner using a 10-d nail rather than the 8-inch spikes because they were shorter and wouldn't go through to the stones. And too, I had to secure the logs for the next phase, and that was to attach the floor joist ledger boards. I didn't want to dislodge the squared-up logs when I nailed the ledger boards to them. When I say nailed, I wasn't going to permanently fasten them with nails; I was just going to use the nails to hold them in place while I drilled holes for the lag screws.

Anyway, it was getting on in the afternoon and I looked forward to a good supper with the "Old Timer". I went down to the creek and washed up.

I climbed into the Jeep to head down the road to supper, but I paused before leaving to admire the work I had done. I felt a sense of pride and accomplishment as the Jeep bounced its way down to the "Old Timer's" cabin.

I knocked on his door, was told to come in. I stepped into the warm room and was greeted pleasantly by the appetizing aroma of corn beef hash and the smell of hot coffee coming from a pot percolating on the wood stove.

My appetite was ravenous and it all tasted so good that I ate more than my share. He was delighted that his fare had gone over so well, but he probably did not realize the amount of physical activity I had so rigorously engaged in had contributed to my heartily consumption.

To be honest, I think anything cooked at that time would have gone over well.

Later, we visited over coffee. He asked if I was taking a load of lumber back up with me, and I said that I was.

"It's getting close to dark," he said. "Perhaps you should spend the night here. You could sleep on that day bed there, and after breakfast I could help you load up."

I was stuffed now and relaxed and the day's activity was beginning to take its toll. I didn't exactly relish wrestling a load of lumber up the windy and bumpy road, and then trying to fix my lean-to in the dark, so I readily accepted his kind offer.

I lay down on the cot, only removing my boots, and went right to sleep and did not wake up until the "Old Timer" was rustling around in the morning putting wood in the stove. I might add that the old fellow could really fix good meals, for that breakfast, like last night's supper was very tasty and filling.

Later he and I together loaded 22 two by eights on the Jeep. I had put the windshield down, and with the seat out, the boards fit easily along that side. We lashed them to the front and rear bumpers. These boards were for the floor joists and the ledger.

The weather being damp and cool had coated the trees with a layer of heavy white frost. Driving up the road under this frosty mantle created an illusion of being part of a very fancy greeting card. It filled me with awe and I was so thankful to be given the opportunity to witness such a spectacular sight. A sight that I knew would last but just a short while for the warm rays of the morning sun was beginning its slow but steady climb up the mountain side. I felt blessed to have come along just at this time to witness such a magnificent wonder of Nature.

⸺⸻❧⸻⸺

I unloaded the boards from the Jeep stacking them at the end of the driveway near the logs. I selected two of the 10 footers out of the lot, and carried one at a time to the site inside the perimeter.

To cover the 20-foot span I planned on butting two of the 10 footers together. These two then would make one ledger board. Both the north and the south wall would have a ledger board fastened to it on the inward side.

I started on the north side. With the hammer, I drove some 10d nails temporarily, just above center of the boards about two feet apart just in far enough so their points stuck out a little way on the other side. These nails were just to hold it place until I got it all leveled and then I would permanently fasten it to the log with lag screws.

I placed the level close by. I started on the left side of the north log by butting the board up against the west log and pounded the first nail into the north log, just far enough in to hold the end of the board and allow it to swivel up or down a bit. I shuffled over to my right keeping a hold of the board. I reached for the level and placed it on the top edge of the board. Moving the board slightly upward I matched the bubble with the mark and then, holding the board steady, I pounded in another nail. The first ledger board was level. I repeated the procedure for the second board, and to my excitement it butted up against the east wall log perfectly. That proved the length was 20 feet. I had been wondering about that. Now to put up the two ledger boards on the south side and I hoped to have the same success.

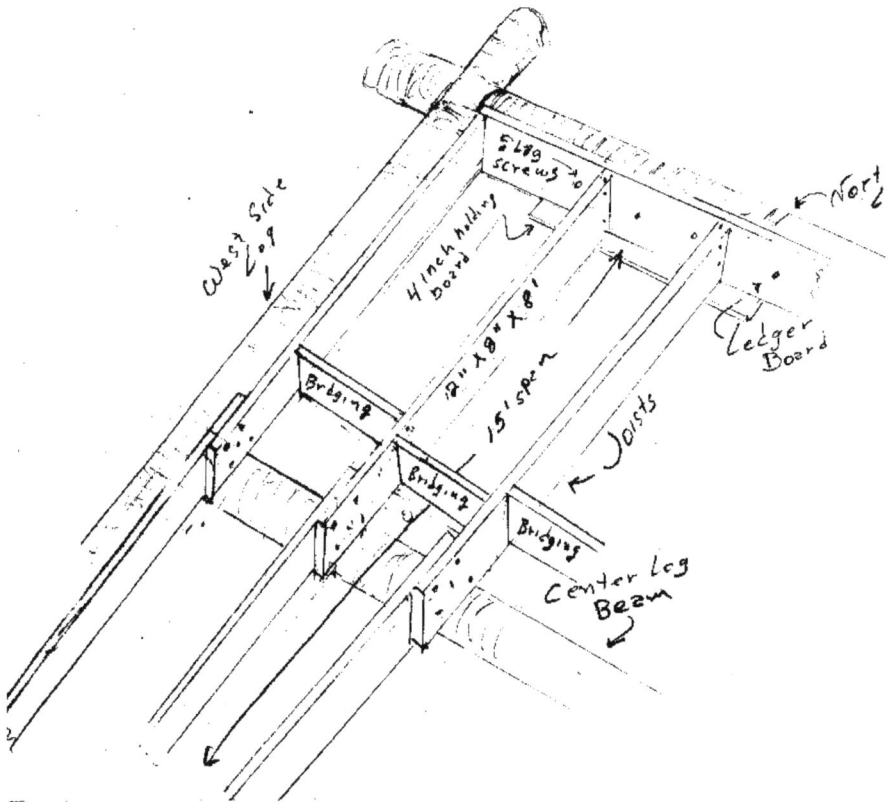

West Side Log

5 Log screws to

4 inch holders Board

12" x 8" x 8'

15' span

North

Ledger Board

Joists

Bridging

Bridging

Bridging

Center Log Beam

Illustrations from the journal of Dan Fields ©1980

I got two more boards from the pile for the south side, and following through using the same methods I had done on the north side, I soon had all ledger boards nailed temporarily in place. I mentioned earlier that I was going to permanently fasten the ledger boards with lag screws. I had brought along a brace and bit with a 1/4-inch bit to drill the pilot holes. I drilled the holes about every two feet and then screwed 3-inch lag screws into them using a socket wrench.

I would have liked to start installing the floor joist, but I could not start until a center beam was installed.

I'll explain that: The boards I had for the joists were 8 footers so to span the 15 feet I planned to use two boards, one end fastened to the ledger on the north side and the other end fastened to the ledger on the south side and they would overlap in the center of the span. But they needed a support where they overlapped. So, a log running east and west as a center support beam would be needed.

I had not allowed for a center support when I cut the logs last year. Can't think of everything, I guess. I could go up above and find a downed tree, cut it up and use it. But, the center log needs to be good and strong, so I opted to go ahead and use one that I had cut last year, leaving me one shy.

Illustrations from the journal of Dan Fields ©1980

It was now getting late into the evening, but I felt like getting this last phase done before cooking supper. I wrestled the log to the center and after measuring it; I cut a notch on the top of each end and slid it underneath the east log and west log.

I braced it up like I did the corners with two stones underneath each end. I had to use the car jack to lift it into the bottom notch, and hold it while I worked the top stone under it while maintaining the top of it level with the bottom of the ledger board. But I did manage and then decided I had had enough for one day and it was time for supper. After all it was nearly dark.

Once I install the floor joists I'll lose my campsite, so after breakfast the next morning I drove down to get a load of boards. I can lay some of them across the joists and have a level place to sleep on. It would be much easier cooking supper on the level than on the ground. There is a lot of good to be said about level places. One has to be living like I do to appreciate those things.

After a couple cups of coffee with the "Old Timer", (he liked having company) he helped me load up the Jeep.

There were no frosted trees this morning to greet me on the way up. But the olive green of the tall pines faded gently into the deep blue of the sky promising a great day to build cabins. I again felt a sense of wonder and appreciation as my vintage Jeep slowly wound its way up the rocky road. Its ability to carry such a heavy load under such harsh conditions amazed me, I was most grateful.

I arrived and pulled into the driveway, but left the boards on the Jeep. I planned to use them later and no sense to move them twice. I went into the perimeter of the logs and studied my next move. The floor joist installing was the next thing to do, so I got busy and carried 22 of them up from the driveway and placed them inside the perimeter.

One thing I *had* thought of was how to hold the joist up against the ledger and nail them in place without their slipping or falling down. So, I had brought with me a 4-inch board about 3 feet long to nail on the bottom side of the ledger board to act as a ledge to hold the joist and prevent it from falling down.

That 4-inch board worked great as a ledge holding up the joists. I would rest one end of the joist on the ledge and the other end on the center beam. After I toenailed the joist in place with 10d nails, I would remove the 4-inch board and nail it further along to hold the next joist. So, I continued on with this method and soon had all of the joists nailed in place.

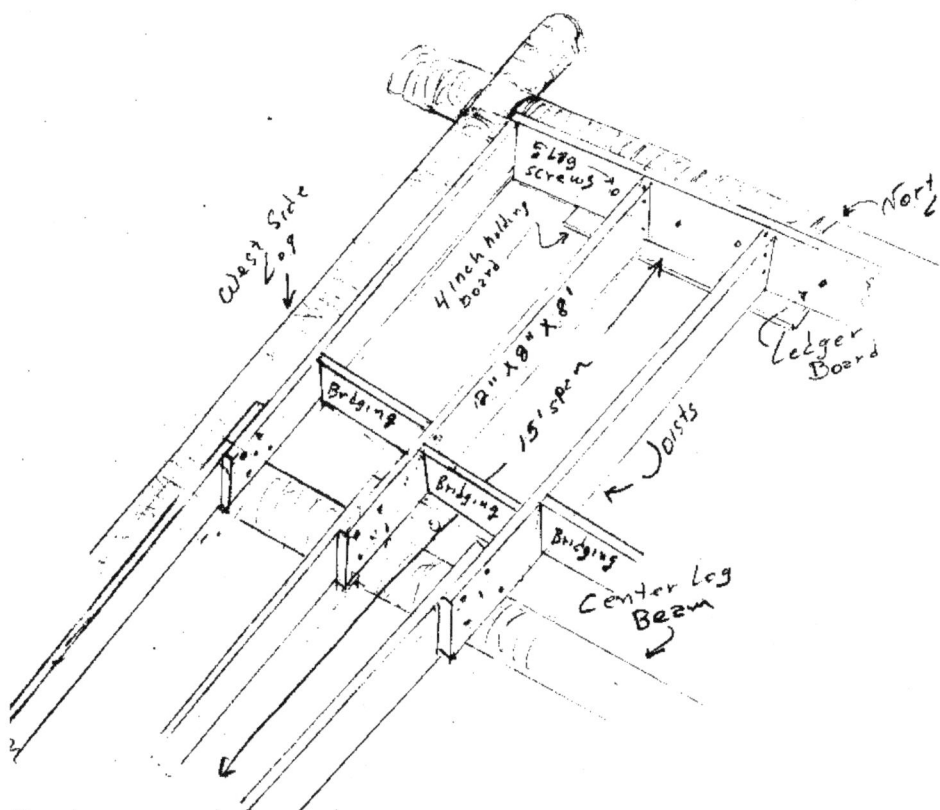

Illustrations from the journal of Dan Fields ©1980

To fasten them where they lay over lapped on the center beam was just a matter of nailing them together and toe nailing them to the beam with 8d nails.

But I had to stop and eat lunch as I was quite hungry and it should give me enough energy to wind up the floor joist project. I settled for a can of pork & beans and that did the trick.

I was not quite finished with the floor joist project yet even though all of them were in. They needed to be bridged up to prevent them from tipping over sometime in the future.

I had several 8 footers left so I sawed out 10 bridging boards into 2-foot lengths to place in between each of the joists as near to the center beam as possible. I staggered them so as to be able to nail them through on each end. The hard part was sawing each one.

That night, while in my sleeping bag, I thought I would never get to sleep. My mind was busy nailing down floorboards and notching logs. But then, somewhere along the way between a log notch and a floorboard I gave up and dropped off to sleep.

The Floor Boards

It was late in the morning when I awoke. I was too excited to have an appetite for I realized that when the last floorboard was nailed down I could start laying more logs. But I knew I wouldn't last long not having something in me, so I opted to have a peanut butter and jelly sandwich (PBJ) washed down with a cup of hot coffee. I went to the creek for the water, lit the stove, and soon was sipping the last cup of coffee after having eaten two sandwiches.

Each row of the floorboards would cover a 20-foot span, so to accomplish that I used 8 footers and 12 footers placed end on end. I started the first row by placing an 8-footer on the joists, nailing it down and then placing a 12-footer and nailing it down, making sure that each end of the floor board where they butted together rested on one half of a floor joist. Out of habit, I made sure I placed each board with its top side up. This was important when I was laying boards on an outside project that were exposed to the elements, not necessarily required here.

Then on the second row I alternated the boards by placing a12 footer on the joists, nailing it down, and then placing an 8-footer and nailing it down. I used 8d nails to fasten them down. I did not have to saw or adjust the length of any floorboard thanks to my being so careful at the start of making sure everything was square and at the proper length.

I had become so engrossed in what I was doing that I had not taken any time to stop and eat lunch.

When I had finished nailing down the last board it was too late in the day to start in on laying down a log or two. So, I had to be satisfied with the day's accomplishments.

While I was down at the stream getting water for my evening meal and while the tea kettle was filling, I looked up at the site, couldn't see from there any of my workings, but I knew that someday soon I'd be here looking up and seeing a log cabin. A sense of urgency crept over me and I had to refrain myself from getting back up there and start laying logs.

But, after eating a wholesome meal, the thought of doing anymore today was out of the question. Settling back in the Jeep seat with a cup of coffee and a cigar, I could tell that the few days of bending; stooping; pounding; lifting; sawing; chopping, and what all, had taken its toll. In fact, a warm sleeping bag was beginning to look very inviting. With the last of the hot water I took a sponge bath and retired for the day. Again, the wind songs of the night lulled me to sleep.

—————⟨✦⟩—————

For six days working steadily I notched and placed the remaining forty logs on the cabin, and it took some effort to mount them, I might add. Getting them up from the driveway in it was laborious as the driveway, from digging it out, had a three-foot bank to get over right off the bat. I pounded two stakes, about 10 feet apart about 6 inches high on top of this bank. I'd lift one end of the log and place it behind a stake. Then I would go to the other end of the log, lift it up and place it behind the other stake. The stakes would hold the log for me while I got on top of the bank. Then I'd lift up one end of the log, walk with it a way, and then go lift the other end, and so on.

Several logs I moved with my block and tackle. The block and tackle had a ratio of 4 to 1, so when I pulled out 4 feet of rope the log had only moved 1 foot, and it took a lot of rope pulling to move the log any appreciable distance. I abandoned it and continued on with the struggle, I just rested more often.

As the walls grew taller so did the lifting distance. It became more difficult to lift one end up and then go and lift up the other end. So, the taller it grew the less logs I could mount in a day. Another thing too, when I had lifted one end of a log that high and rested it on the protruding end of the top log and went to lift the other end, I had to stay clear in case it fell off.

I did all of the raising of the logs from the east sidewall and the north sidewall. The south side was too far off the ground, and the ground on the west side dropped off down to the creek.

Fortunately, most of the logs were very straight, but several of them bowed a little bit and those took a little more time. To straighten out the bow I sawed 6 kerf cuts 2 inches deep and about an inch apart on top of the bow.

Then as I drove the spike down it pulled the log into the kerf cuts and thus straightened it out.

On cutting the notches, after raising the log to the top of the wall, I'd study it to see which is the best way for it to lie. After determining that, I'd turn it over and do the notching. As the walls became higher I could no longer keep the tools on the floorboards and reach down for them.

So, to keep them handier and within reach I placed the 3-foot board, used for holding the joists, cross ways in the corner one end held up by the space between the logs, and the other end I tacked it into a log. This board afforded me a level shelf, not too wide, but it served the purpose.

To make the notch, I would use the small saw first making a series of kerf cuts and then

Illustrations from the journal of Dan Fields ©1980

chisel and /or hatchet it out. I'd do both ends of the log that way and then roll it over and fit its notch into the previous cut notch of the log beneath it.

After checking that it was level and straight, I pounded an 8-inch spike in each corner and in the center of the 15-foot log I would pound a 12-inch spike. On the 20-foot span, I would pound two 12-inch spikes about seven feet from each of the corners. Maybe I didn't have to do that, but I did anyway.

I used a seven-pound short-handled sledgehammer to pound in the spikes. I would straddle the logs and the bark on them was very course and hard on a pair of Jeans. One morning when it was very cool I put on a pair of corduroy pants hoping to break the chill, and by noon they were nearly in shreds. So, I learned to stick to the heavy denim Jeans.

As the work progressed and the walls grew taller, I found it more difficult to get in and out of the cabin. To get in or out I had to climb over the walls each time, and when it got up to around five feet high I decided that it was time to make a doorway.

Illustrations from the journal of Dan Fields ©1980

For the door, I planned to use two by fours and two by eights for the doorframe, with an opening of around thirty inches. To get the exact measurements I laid 8 two by fours on the floor, measured the width of them and added to that measurement the thickness of 2 two by eights.

I marked out the total width on the top of the west wall log. On each end of that width mark, I nailed 2 - two by fours, on either side, leveling them to make sure they were straight up and down. These then would serve two purposes. One, they would give me a straight line to follow when cutting out the opening, and, two, they would hold up the log ends once the section is cut out.

The opening was to be on the west wall but not in the center, but to the left of center. I wanted the stove to sit in the center.

Using the big saw, I placed it against the two by four on the left. It didn't matter which side I started on. So, to make the cuts I sawed on the right edge of the left two by four, and sawed on the left edge of the right two by four.

When I cut out the first one it fell inside and just missed my big toe. So, on the rest of them, I was much more cautions.

After making the opening, I framed the sawed edges with the two by eight's, including the top of the frame, fastening them in place with 10d nails. The height of the door opening was, I believe, 6 feet 9 inches. I then removed the two by four supports. Before I laid the other logs on that wall that were to butt up against the door frame, I think there were two of them, I measured and sawed them to length first before putting them in place. I notched the ends and nailed the other end to the doorframe. The log on the other side of the doorframe was of course a shorter log, but it required notching and nailing to the frame.

When I finished with the door opening I went on then and did the opening on the south sidewall for the window. For the window, I had

acquired two French doors and each one was seven feet high. The panes of glass in them would be fine for the window but the tops and bottoms had too much board in them. So, I cut them down leaving me with two five-foot long windows.

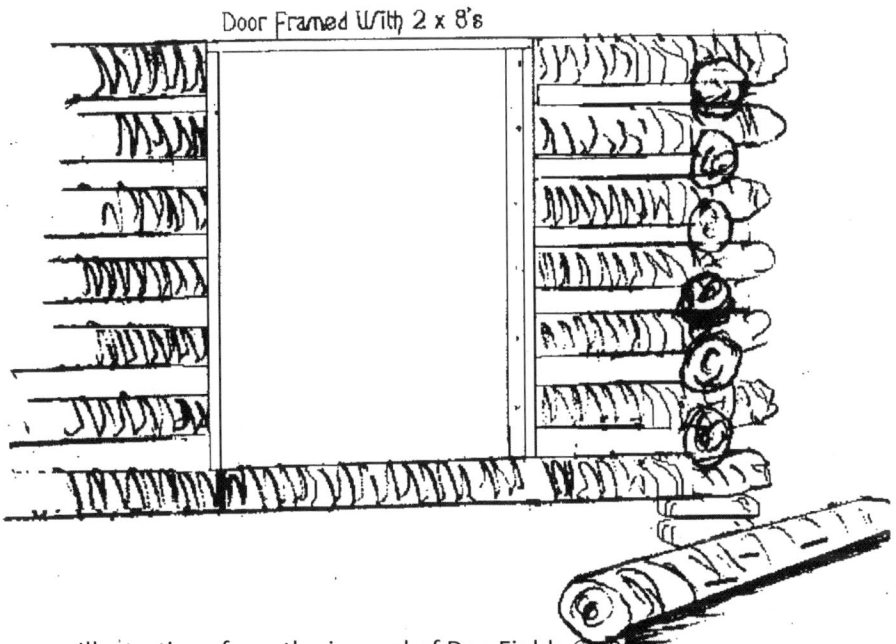

Door Framed With 2 x 8's

Illustrations from the journal of Dan Fields ©1980

I measured the place on the side of the wall allowing space to put a horizontal log between the two windows. I braced the logs with two by four supports as I had done with the door opening.

I not only cut out the space, framed it, but I also installed the windows. It was really getting to resemble a cabin.

As with cutting the logs that butted up against the doorframe, I applied the same method with the window frame, cutting them to a shorter length. And that was a real relief not having to always lift full-length logs.

By now 15 days had passed, and the roof was the next project on my mental list. I had hauled up all the remaining lumber from below so the rafters and roof boards were all stacked neatly in the driveway. I decided on a ridge board to tie the rafters into, but to put one up that high and to cross a 20-foot span had me baffled at first. I knew it would bow if it weren't thick enough and if I spliced several together it might be too heavy and bulky for me to handle it, and still it might bow.

I was relaxing with a cup of coffee when suddenly an idea crossed my mind. Why not do the ridge in sections, say an 8-foot or 10-foot two by four. That seemed to be an easier solution. Now if I could figure out a way to hold it up, then attach the rafters, which would then hold it up, and then add another section.

So, I leaned back in the Jeep seat, sipped on a cup of coffee and got my mind busy working on a solution. First of all, if I were to use an 8 foot two by four as the first section, I would need some support to hold it up, say on the west end. That could be accomplished by a ridge board support nailed to the outside of the west log wall and extending upward 5 feet. I could cut out a slot at the top of it to accommodate the end of the ridge board. That would be simple enough.

But figuring out a way of holding up the other end of the ridge board section would require a little more ingenuity, and as I recall the height of the ridge was around 14 feet, high. I had no lumber that long, but I could splice something and brace it up some way.

Then in my mind popped the purlin logs. There were four of them and not too heavy, and I could use three of them to form a tripod.

But then it occurred to me. How could I reach up to the top of the tripod and place the ridge on it? So, I dismissed that idea

The purlins were still in my mind, and then the solution hit me in the head like a lightning bolt.

"The purlins are the solution, you Dummy," I yelled out loud. "Not as a tripod but as a purlin. Put the purlins in place and put boards across them to stand on and then you can easily erect a 5-foot brace to hold up the end section of the ridge board." So, I did that next.

⸻ ❧ ⸻

Installing the Purlins

There were four of them and easy to handle, not like the heavy logs I was used to. I lifted each one up end at a time spacing them four feet apart starting at the west wall. Since they were seventeen feet long they extended out past the wall by two feet, but I lined them up on one end even with the top log and cut off the extra two feet from the other end. I cut notches in the purlins and the logs so the purlins were flush with the top of the logs, and spiked the ends down using the 8-inch spikes.

Taking about six of the 8-inch roof boards, I placed them across the purlins, thus giving me something to stand on, and that would allow me easy reach to the ridge board and also when attaching the rafters.

Then I nailed a ridge board support on the outside center of the east wall and made sure it was plumb straight up and down, and that it measured 5 feet from the top of the slot to the top of the log. I did the same with one more on the west wall

For the first section of the ridge board, I selected a straight 8 foot two by four. One end would be held up by the slotted ridge board support, say on the west wall, and to hold up the other end of the ridge board I sawed an 8-inch board down to 5 feet, cut a notch out of one end of it.

I placed one end of the ridge board in the slot of the ridge board support and the other end in the slot of the board I had just cut, the end support board. The end support board, being 8 inches wide, was wide enough to stand alone without tipping over while I lined the ridge board up with the other wall with a piece of string.

After getting it plumb and making sure it was five feet high, I nailed the bottom of the end support board to the purlin it stood on to prevent it from accidentally slipping away. I

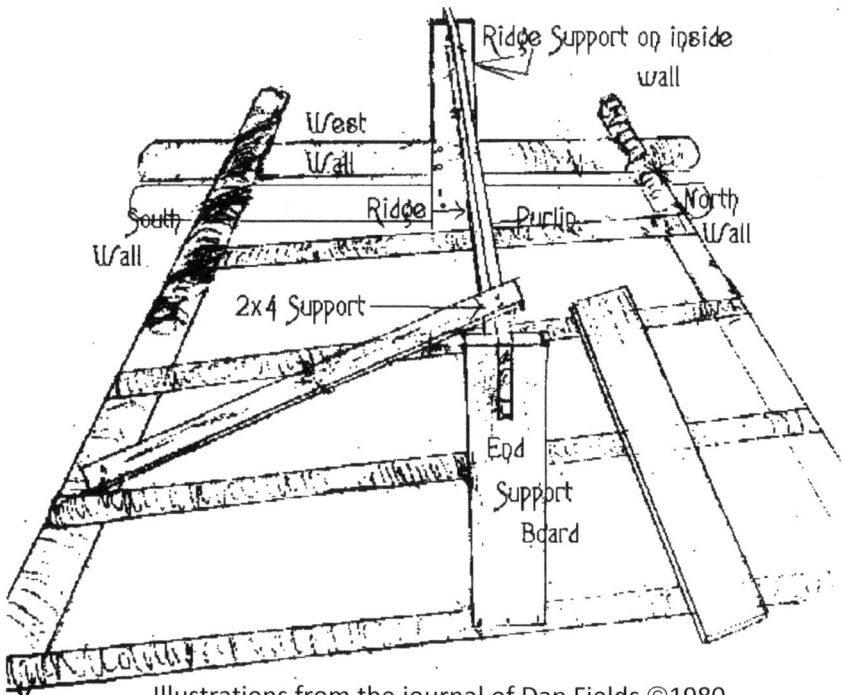

Illustrations from the journal of Dan Fields ©1980

then took one of the rafters and laid one end of it across the ridge board, just above the end support board, and the other end ran across to the top log on the south wall. I nailed it temporarily in place on both ends, allowing me something solid to pound against when I nailed the first rafter.

After figuring out the angle at which to cut the end of the rafter that butted up against the ridge board, I cut all of them down below with a handsaw. I had no sawhorses instead I dropped the tailgate of the Jeep and used it. I also pre-pounded nails in the rafters with just the points protruding. I leaned all of the rafter boards up against the purlins to avoid having to go down below for them.

I did not notch too deeply on the rafter as it was only a two by four, but I notched deeper on the log, deep enough so that the rafter fit flush on top of the log. By doing this the roof boards would also fit flush and would not have a gap to fill in. That would save quite a bit of effort later on and too; it would keep critters and birds out.

I placed the rafters every 2 feet and the idea of the end support board went well. It had to be moved only twice. In the course of a day, the rafters were in. And so, another day of toil ended successfully, and I again enjoyed a hot meal of pork & beans and crackers. I missed having a table though so I stood two short logs on end, (the ones I had sawed out for the doorway) and that worked fairly well.

<hr />

The Roof Boards

It was another gorgeous day and after a hearty breakfast I was ready for the next task at hand. Putting on the roof boards.

The roof boards were the last of the long pieces of lumber I would have to handle. They were ten footers and twelve footers, and six were already up on the purlins that were being used as a walkway. Sixty in all were needed, enough, I had figured, to cover the entire roof and give a decent over hang on both ends. I would not be out of lumber entirely though, as there was a bunch left which I would use for the gable ends.

I had never boarded up a roof before so I didn't really know the right or wrong way to do it. Should I start laying the boards from the bottom ends of the rafters and work my way up to the ridge? But what if upon reaching the ridge and the last board extended out over the ridge, it would be difficult to rip the long board down to a narrower width even if I had a rip saw.

I decided I should start laying the roof boards from the ridge and work down so if any hung over it would be all right and no ripping required. I could build a trough out of two boards and turn it upside down on the ridge, and then work my way down.

That decided I selected two of the 12 footers and using the 8d nails I constructed a trough, and then did the same with 2 of the 10 footers. As they were heavy I lugged them one at a time to the north sidewall, it being closer to the ground, and slid each one upon to the rafters. Climbing in between the rafters and standing on the boards laid on the purlins, I inched the two troughs up over the ridge. The tops of the two ridge board supports were square, or straight across, so I had to saw them off the same angle as that of the trough.

Before nailing them in place with 8d nails, I measured each end for an equal over hang.

I carried all of the roof boards up from the driveway and leaned them against the top logs so I could reach them easily from up on the roof. I leaned the required number of boards on the south side and the remainder on the north side, which was less because I had several of the boards on the purlins, separating them as I went by placing the 10 footers on the left and the 12 footers on the right. So, when I was on the roof I knew where the different sizes were.

I filled my nail pouch full of 8d nails and climbed up the north side using the space between the logs as a ladder. The boards that lay across the purlins provided me with a catwalk, although I had to watch my step. I started placing the boards on the south side alternating the lengths as I went. This method of starting first at the ridge proved to be most awkward. I had to shift the boards on the catwalk around and then I was climbing over the rafters. The first several layers were not that difficult as the ridge was 5 feet high and I could walk under it, but as I progressed, the height diminished preventing me from walking under it so I had to hop over the rafters a lot to change positions.

After I had laid four rows I changed my method of operation and climbed up on top of the boards. Although I was working in a squatting position, I made better progress. As I neared the edge of the rafters, the situation got a little precarious, as the south side was rather high off of the ground. So, I had to be extra careful.

Illustrations from the iournal of Dan Fields ©1980

I was just about out of nails and in need of a break and some sort of refreshment. And too, I had worked up a tremendous thirst and a good cold drink from the stream would be mighty tasty. So, I climbed down from the north side and took a little time off.

After a good break and a hearty snack, I returned to the roof and commenced laying boards on the north side. For the first four rows, I could sit on the south sideboards and not have to hop over any rafters. Before I had gone too far though I decided I better retrieve the boards from off the purlins while I had space in which to maneuver them. So, I wrestled them up and laid them out across the rafters.

I continued slowly working my way downward as I had done on the other side and it went fast enough. It was late in the afternoon when I finished nailing the last board down, and I was really glad about that because my back was beginning to kill me from all of the bending over.

Climbing off the north wall this time was a little more difficult than it had been before, and it wasn't because of my back. Here to fore I'd just go straight down the outside wall using the space in the logs for a toehold, but this time I had an overhang to cross over and no handhold. So, I had to slide down on my stomach backwards and grope around with my boots for the space in the logs and wished that I had had the foresight to construct a ladder.

That night for the first time I slept indoors, and I must say that I had become so accustomed to looking up at the stars that I felt like something was missing.

———————◆———————

Early the next day I put the seat back in the Jeep and raised up the windshield and drove down to the hardware store in the small town about twenty miles away. I purchased 3 rolls of tar paper; 4 rolls of roofing; about 10 pounds of roofing nails; 2 gate hinges; a hasp; three firing strips; a pad lock, and two gate handles. Then on to the grocery store for some more grub and some fresh bread, the last of my moldy loaf I had fed to the Magpies.

On returning, I stopped in to visit the "Old Timer" and was surprised to find a pick-up truck in the clearing where I had stored my lumber. I walked up to his door and he and the driver were carrying out a wood-burning stove. I backed out of the way and they sat it down a short distance out.

Without going into a lot of detail of what we discussed, a friend had donated a newer wood stove to the "Old Timer" and they were setting the old one out. And to my good fortune, I came into a wood cook stove, and I had some help in loading it. I stood the rolls of roofing on end and dropped the tailgate to make room for the stove.

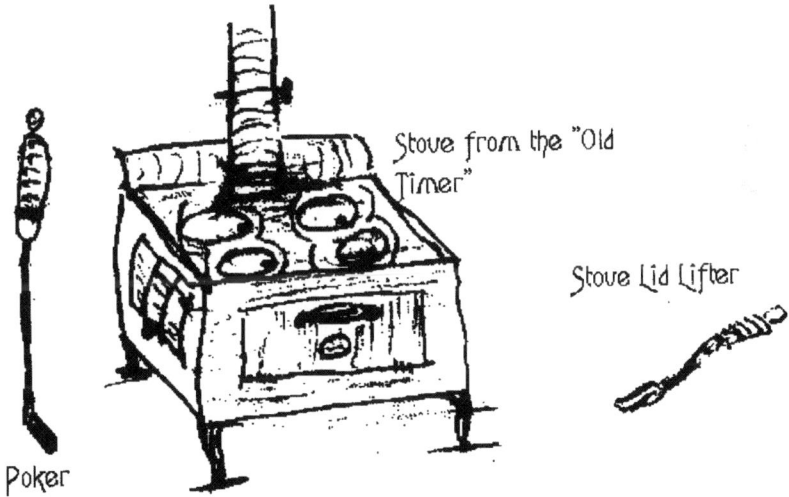

Stove from the "Old Timer"

Stove Lid Lifter

Poker

Illustrations from the iournal of Dan Fields ©1980

The "Old Timer" even rode up with me to help get it into my cabin. And of course, I had to show him all of my accomplishments and I do believe that he was impressed. He also helped me carry the rolls of roofing into the cabin.

With a stove sitting in the room it was really taking on the shape of "home." But still ahead was the roofing and of course, the chinking.

He refused a ride back down insisting on walking it, but before he left he gave me some good advice on roofing. He said that when I carry up the first couple of roofing strips take'em way up near the top and roll'em out there, because they're going to slide down on you. So, if you roll'em out near the bottom they'll fall off to the ground and maybe tear. And it might be a good idea to nail some sticks or a board along the ends of the rafters to stop'em from sliding' off. "Just thought I'd tell ya," and then he left as though he had something pressing to do. Maybe he wanted to get back and admire his newly acquired stove.

I decided that after a bite to eat I would tackle the job of building a ladder. I used two Aspens and a third one I cut in 2-foot lengths. I cut out notches and nailed the cross pieces in place with 8d nails. (I was now an expert on notching). It didn't have to be too tall as the north side was close enough to the ground, not like that of the south side, but I did want it to be strong enough to hold me up. And it was.

I took the old timers advice and nailed sticks to the ends of every other rafter. Then I removed the wrapper from the tarpaper and rolled it out on the cabin floor. I needed a 22-foot strip so the cabin being 20 feet I overlapped two feet and cut it out with my pocketknife, and rolled up the cut-off piece.

The ladder was in place; my nail pouch filled this time with roofing nails, and the hammer in the loop. So, with the roll on my shoulder I climbed up and placed it on the roof so it wouldn't roll off while I stepped off the ladder. I took it up almost to the ridge and to the west end. I had unrolled about half of it when it began to slide. I laid the rolled end down and got over to the other end and stopped its slide. Had I started it at the edge and rather than higher up it would have definitely slid off onto the ground. So, I offered a silent "thank you," to the "Old Timer".

I found out though it did not have the tendency to slide down as readily if I unrolled while heading slightly downward. Finally, I had it fully unrolled, but it was at an angle and about 4 feet at the closest to the bottom edge of the roof board. I hopped over it and at the center I took hold of the upper edge, my hands being about three feet apart, and relying on the sticks, just in case, I slowly began to wiggle it and jiggle it. I slowly moved it downward straightening it out as I went until it rested firmly up against the sticks. What a life safer they were. I nailed roofing nails in the bottom and the top edge about a foot apart.

For some reason, the next strips gave me no trouble at all as the first one had done. I over lapped the first strip by 6 inches and placed nails only in the bottom edge because the top edge would be held down when I nailed the next strip over it and I continued on laying four strips.

The rolls were 36 inches wide so by overlapping 6 inches each strip would cover 30 inches. Four strips then would cover the 120 inches (10 feet), which would reach the ridge. So, the top edge of the fourth strip went just to the ridge.

Going next to the south side I nailed sticks on the rafter ends, leaving those in place on the north side because they would be needed when I started laying the roofing.

I decided though to lay some roofing on the north side rather than tar paper the south side, just to see how it would go. Although it was heavier, the same technique worked out as well as it did with the tarpaper. I applied three strips of the roofing and then resumed laying the tarpaper on the south side finishing it up to the ridge. The last strip of tarpaper did not have to be very wide so I cut a strip about 8 inches wide and centered it down the ridge and nailed it down on both edges

Although it was well into the afternoon, I was on a roll and wanted to finish the roofing project so I continued on by placing four strips of roofing on the south side.

I then laid the fourth strip on the north side. For the ridge, I cut the last strip, about eight inches wide, and laid it down the center, nailing it good on both edges. The roofing was finished.

I had plenty of roofing and tarpaper left over in the last rolls.

━━━━━➤◦◄━━━━

It was just getting dark when I limped down the ladder. I was too tired to cook anything so I just munched on some crackers and drank creek water. I did get out the Jeep seat allowing me a comfortable place to rest up.

Later, though I mustered up enough strength to light the Coleman stove and warmed up a can of Boyardee. And to my delight, I could use the newly acquired wood stove as a table, so I discarded the logs. I rested back in the seat, being very tired, and suddenly realized that I had been working steadily for the last 18 days. The thought made me even more tired. I had not bathed or shaved, I had washed up a bit on occasion, so I thought that tomorrow I would heat enough water to wash up. I might even shave. Maybe I should put on some different clothes too, at least clean ones.

That night brought with it quite a downpour. For the first time, I heard raindrops on my roof. And then the words came to me from Thoreau. "A Roof Impervious to Rain." That quote remained in my mind as the rainstorm settled down to a gentle pitter-patter and its mesmerizing rhythm soon had me fast asleep.

———————✕❋✕———————

I cleaned up the next morning, shaved, put on some clean clothes, and even changed my socks. I took the dirty clothes down to the creek, (I started calling it a creek now instead of a stream) and found a spot where the water was running swift and staked them down into it. The swift current should have them cleaned up in no time.

I was now running out of time, as I had to be back on the job Monday and today was Friday.

I mulled over what still had to be done and I would have to establish priorities.

There was the door to build and install. The gables needed closing in and I had decided that I had enough boards to do that. The chinking, which required material that I did not have; cement and sand, could wait. And there were things to do ahead, like hooking up the stove and cutting a hole in the roof for the pipe.

I dismissed thinking of everything but the door and the gables. Those I could do with the tools and materials at hand.

Using the firing strips as doorstops I nailed them inside the doorframe. Then I built the door with the two by fours and braced it across its top and bottom with cross pieces. The door had to be off the floor in order for it to open and close so I took a stick with the thickness of about a quarter of an inch, broke it in half and placed it on the floor in the door opening. I lifted the door in place resting on the sticks, and it fit so snugly that it needed no bracing.

Now for the gate hinges. I drilled the pilot holes with the brace and bit and fastened the hinges in place with lag screws and got them in real tight. And then I fastened on a handle, and removed the two sticks. I was really proud of my workmanship, but it was soon shattered and short lived. For when I tried to open the door it wouldn't budge. Then it dawned on me what was wrong. I did not bevel the edge of the door, the edge opposite to the hinge. So, to get it open I had to remove the hinges and then pull the door straight out. To bevel the edge of a door, one normally uses a plane, but of course I had no such tool. I had a hatchet, chisel, a cross cut saw, and of course my pocket knife.

Then I came up with the idea of the method I had used on the notches. Take the saw and go down the edge of the door cutting kerf marks every half-inch at an angle of about a quarter of an inch deep. Then take the chisel and pry them out.

Using a board as a straight edge, I drew a line a quarter of an inch from the edge down the length of the door.

I sawed away and with that done, I chiseled out the cuts. I lifted the door and placed it back on top of the sticks. I again fastened the hinges, not with all of the screws, but just enough to test it. I removed the sticks from underneath the door and pulled on the handle. The door was snug, but it did open. There were a few protruding edges that needed smoothing out, but they were hard to see with the doorstop in place. I pried loose the doorstop giving me lighter so I could see more clearly where the hang-ups were. I marked where each one was with a pencil and then opened the door. I whittled them off as best I could with my pocketknife. The door did open and close much better. I abandoned that project making a mental note to bring up a rasp and sandpaper on my next trip up here. It will have to do for now. I screwed in the remainder of the lag screws, and then replaced the doorstop.

Illustrations from the journal of Dan Fields ©1980

Opening the door once again, I stepped outside and installed the hasp and another handle. Other than needing a little sanding here and there, the door was in and finished.

The Gables

The gables were the last items to be installed that would then completely enclose the cabin. I had the last of the boards in the driveway, and hoped that my figuration had been accurate. Before doing any cutting, I decided to take the tape measure and double check my old figures. The total length to cover on either side of the center ridge support board was 90 inches, and dividing that by the actual width of 7.5 inches, I would need 12 boards 5 feet long.

I sawed 12 of the 10-foot boards in half giving me 24 – five footers for both sides of the gables. Making several trips I carried them all into the cabin, as I needed a good level spot on which to lay them.

I laid 12 out on the floor making a rectangle of 5 feet (60 inches) by 90 inches and these were to make up one end of the gables, say the west end. I drew a diagonal chalk line from the upper right-hand corner to the bottom left hand corner, giving me the correct angle and length of each board. After sawing out each one, I used the bottom right of the rectangle boards for the left side gable and the upper left side of the rectangle, reversing the boards, for the right side of the gable.

I repeated this method in measuring, marking, and cutting out the gable boards for the east wall. Using 8d nails I secured them to the rafters and the logs.

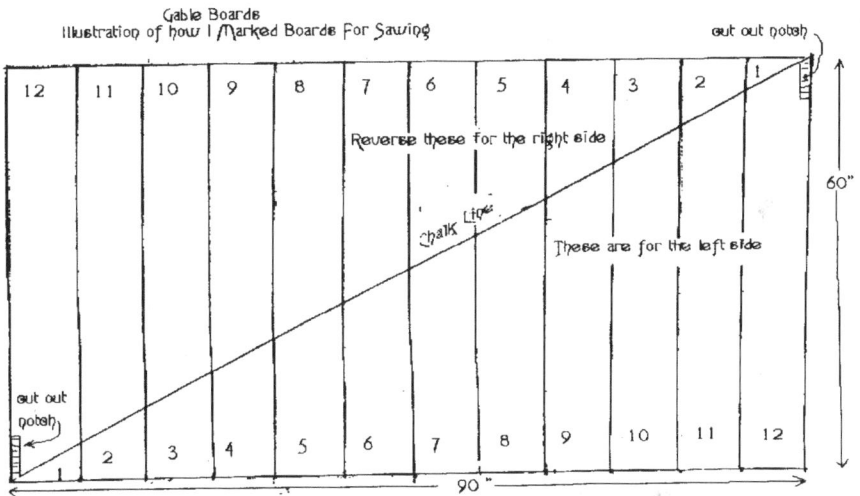

Gable Boards
Illustration of how I Marked Boards For Sawing

cut out notch

| 12 | 11 | 10 | 9 | 8 | 7 | 6 | 5 | 4 | 3 | 2 | 1 |

Reverse these for the right side

60"

chalk line

These are for the left side

cut out notch

| 1 | 2 | 3 | 4 | 5 | 6 | 7 | 8 | 9 | 10 | 11 | 12 |

90"

Illustrations from the journal of Dan Fields ©1980

Gables Nailed Up

Illustrations from the journal of Dan Fields ©1980

121

The next day before leaving I wanted to lock up the cabin, but there was no door latch so I made a mental note to bring one up on my next trip.

I left the cabin then and returned to my job. The following Friday afternoon, I returned, this time my wife accompanied me. She was really impressed with my accomplishments, for when she had seen the place last, it was just an undeveloped wilderness.

We had the Jeep loaded with so many things that one can only imagine, but to name a few: Sleeping bags; 2 buckets; stove pipe and thimble; folding chairs; a folding table; pots and pans; food; 4 sacks of cement; some wire; window screens; rubber gloves, and four plastic pans. Two of the pans to use for mixing cement, and two pans for washing and rinsing dishes.

The first order of business was the hooking up of the stove. I moved the stove around until I found the right spot. I tied a small nut to a length of string, kind of a make shift plumb bob, and using my ladder to climb up on, I held the string up against the ceiling and where the nut hung in the center of the stove pipe opening, I placed an X there on the ceiling. Then I drove a nail up through the ceiling extending out through the roof.

Nut Attached to String

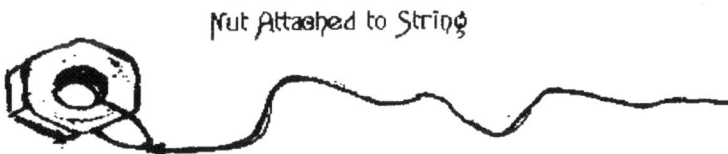

Illustrations from the iournal of Dan Fields ©1980

Taking my ladder, brace and bit, and key hole saw, I climbed up on the roof and drew a circle, using the nail as the center, a little larger than the diameter of a stove pipe, I drilled some holes all around the circle and then evened them up with the key hole saw.

I slipped the thimble down into the hole. Went back inside and fitted three or four lengths of pipe up from the stove into the thimble. I returned to the roof with two lengths of stovepipe, wire, hammer, pliers, and a couple of nails. I fitted the pipe over the thimble. I pounded a nail upon the ridge and one in the end of a rafter and wired the pipe to them both to prevent the pipe from being blown over.

That evening we tried out the stove and I had my first home cooked meal. It was a lot better than some of the fare I had been cooking up.

The next morning after breakfast was the chinking project. I had not brought up any sand as there was a good-sized sand bar down in our creek, and, using the 2 buckets, I laboriously, by many trips, hauled up sand. I dumped each bucket of sand at the edge of the driveway and stopped when I guessed we had enough.

To fill in the gap between the logs and save

on cement, we collected all the downed Aspen we could find and even cut a few small ones, and wedged them in between the logs. Some we nailed in place. After that, we went around each outside wall and pounded 8d nails about a foot apart at the top of each log to hold in the cement. Even if the cement cracked, the nails would hold it in place.

That took all of the morning so after lunch we started mixing the cement. We each had a pair of rubber gloves and a plastic pan, and 1 pineapple can. I cannot recall the exact parts of each used, but I think it was 1 cement to 8 sand, and enough water to make it pasty. Our measuring device was the pineapple can.

Illustrations from the journal of Dan Fields ©1980

So, we mixed it up in the plastic pans and with rubber gloves on, we applied it by hand to the logs. I made many trips to the creek for water, and a few more for sand, but by day's end, the chinking was done. Now the cabin was completely enclosed.

That evening after dark, I stood out in the driveway looking up at the cabin. The soft lamplight flowed out through the windows penetrating the nightfall that here to fore had never seen such a sight. And I was the creator of it all. The aroma of pine smoke summoned me back inside assuring me of a warm hearth and a hot cup of coffee. And too, the roof was impervious to rain.

Post Script

Our family grew larger over the years to include three boys and a girl, and when school had let out my wife would take them up to the cabin to spend most of the summer.

The third boy was born late in February, so when she took the three to the cabin in June, he was still an infant. For his sleeping arrangements, she placed him in the wheelbarrow. It proved very convenient when he needed to be moved around.

By the time the daughter was born in June of the next year we took a baby bed up for her.

As they got older we installed four bunk beds against the east wall.

Later then as they all got a little older; we realized the cabin with its one room was just too small, so I added a kitchen on the south side. Not with logs this time. I framed it in. That went much faster and much less work, as it entailed no heavy lifting. I had plenty of roofing material left over for it. I moved the cook stove into the kitchen and later added a sheet metal heating stove in its place.

Because of the bark left on the logs, (which I learned later that I should have peeled as soon as I had cut them down) the room was dark, so I lined them with light colored paneling. I laid plywood on the purlins and placed insulation on top of that.

Also, I added a small porch onto the west wall using small Lodge Pole pines and boards, and an outhouse just below the driveway.

I of course, had to stay in town during the week because of my job, but I would drive up on Friday evenings with the Jeep (a Wagoneer now because of the family size) full of groceries, and something special for each kid. After supper and the dishes done, we would all hike up the road, where we had been many times, but never grew tired of it.

After dark, we would clear off the table and play Rummy. Then when all were in bed, I'd get out a Hardy Boy's book, and by lamplight, read them about the Boy's adventures.

During the week, my wife had various activities planned to keep the kids busy, although they still had time to play. Each child had a spiral ring notebook. My wife would take them on nature walks pointing out the various wild plants that grew there, the edible ones and the ones not so edible. The kids then would draw, as best they could, the plants in the notebooks indicating the color of each part. When they returned to the cabin they'd get out their crayons and fill in the colors. They learned a lot on how to stay alive in the woods. I guess if my kids were ever lost in the woods, by the time they were found they would have gained weight. To quote Thoreau again, "People starve to death while trampling food under foot."

All three kids learned how to cook on a wood-burning stove. They learned how important it is to keep the wood box, and the water bucket filled.

When the third boy and the girl were still in diapers, when my wife changed them during the day, she would throw them into the heating stove. The next morning when the cabin was cool, she'd light the diapers, now dry, jump back into bed, and in about twenty minutes the chill of the night was broken.

Further Post Script

Times changed, the kids got older and had school activities. My wife had a good job offer that she couldn't turn down. So, we found ourselves spending less and less time at the cabin. One day a person approached me and wanted to purchase it.

He desired a place away from it all where he could live in private with no close neighbors. After some deep and profound family discussions, we relented and sold it to the person.

To respect his privacy, I have deliberately left out names and places. He may not have purchased the best cabin in the west with many amenities, but the one he purchased definitely had a Roof Impervious to Rain.

Illustrations from the iournal of Dan Fields ©1980

A Near Death Experience

on my

Snowshoe Trip

Up Bard Creek

October 1959

By

Dan Fields

A NEAR DEATH EXPERIENCE

There I was alone, miles from nowhere at the base of timber line, in deep snow, boots full of water, no sleeping bag, unable to go any farther, and the freezing temperature of the night was fast approaching.

The soft snow crunched under the snowshoes as I made my way on the old mining road along Bard Creek. It was uphill and the sun had come out melting the crust of the snow making the trip more difficult. None-the-less, I was determined to make it to Lee Minton's Timber Line Cabin and spend a few days writing on my short stories.

It was a Sunday morning, the first week of October 1959 and the mountains were heavy with snow from an unusually early and wet storm. Lee Minton was staying below at his Whispering Pines cabin on Bard Creek, quite some distance from his timberline cabin, and was to expect me back Friday evening at around five o'clock. If I didn't show by then, he was to follow my snowshoe trail, bringing his toboggan sled, food, blankets, and first-aid supplies.

When he bade me good-bye and fair journey, he looked rather quizzically at the sky and told me I should most likely have good weather and should be at the Timberline Cabin by 2 o'clock. With these last words, he lifted up my pack, and I put my arms through the straps. It fit snugly against my back for I had arranged the week's supply of food so no sharp edges would rub me. I put the binocular strap around my neck, picked up my 30-30 carbine, and was off on my trek.

The first leg of my journey consisted of a steep climb that required my stopping often for breath. By the time, I reached the top of the hill the sun had warmed up the fall air until the heavy parka I was wearing became uncomfortable. I shrugged it off, secured it to the pack, and continued on up the steep road.

Because of the early freakish snowstorm, the snow at this point was topped with brackish-brown Aspen leaves. A most unusual sight to see, for the Aspens usually shed their leaves before the first snow, and before shedding the leaves, present a scene of beauty resembling melted gold streaming from each limb.

The road now leveled off somewhat allowing an easier pace, but because the sun was melting the crust of the snow, my snowshoes were sinking down about six inches, and too, the soft-wet snow clung to the webbing making the snowshoes heavier than they should be. Under the trees in the shade however, where the sun did not reach, was the hard crust that helped compensate for the lost time.

Along the road area were many blue jays and camp robbers flying about. Tracks of various animals galore crisscrossed the road and disappeared into the depths of the forest.

Beaver Dam Cabin

After shuffling along for about an hour and a half, the road leveled off and I arrived at a cabin sitting on the right side just about twenty feet off the road that Lee Minton referred to as the Beaver Dam Cabin. It was owned by a Bill Blair of Idaho Springs, and sometimes Lee called it the Blair's Cabin. It faces a wide and flat meadow to the left of the road where the Beaver have diverted Bard Creek with their dams. Three small lakes spot the meadow but will change their position year after year depending on the activity of the beaver.

I went to the porch of the cabin and removed my gear and placed my rifle carefully against the wall. I sat down on an inverted 5-gallon can, ate some chocolate and lit a cigar. It tasted great and I thought that one should never be without a good tasting cigar. I looked at my watch. It was 10:30. I had traveled an hour and a half over a trail that should normally have taken only 40 minutes under better snow conditions and that term of better snow conditions should have registered in my mind as I still had quite a distance to go, but it didn't.

I broke off several icicles hanging from the edge of the roof and munched on them for water, and began to ponder ahead to my next major stop and perhaps lunch. This wasn't my first trip over this road and I knew it quite well. I decided the next stop would be at the abandoned Murmuring Pines Cabin. Depending on the road conditions, I estimated that it would be about a two-hour hike from where I was sitting. A canned spaghetti casserole would be filling and easy to prepare.

Having quenched my thirst and eaten enough chocolate for some quick energy, I fastened the snowshoes to my boots. I swung the pack and rifle to my shoulder and continued on my journey. The road was still level which helped my progress

As I crunched on along the road the birds were still fluttering about looking for what little scraps of food they could find. Now and then a gray squirrel would voice his loud and monotonous "chirp chip" letting me know in no uncertain terms his disapproval of my being there.

Bard Creek Mill

I shuffled on for a half a mile or so. The road became steeper for a little way. Rounding the crest of the small rise, I saw the familiar buildings of the Bard Creek Mill. It had long been abandoned, but the present owner, an old fellow, still has his hopes and dreams of finding a rich vein of gold. Massive timbers hold up the huge Mill structure. Several buildings making up the mill site are scattered over the hillside. The office, which is still in good shape and usable; the blacksmith shop; the mule barn, and, of course, the mine shaft, which I could not see from here, but I knew it was there alongside the blacksmith shop, and the opening of the shaft had long since caved in.

I continued on past the mill and shuffled my snowshoes a little more laboriously now because of the softening snow and the steep hill that rose from behind the mill. The temperature was rising and was nearly 50 degrees making the crust, even in the shade, soft and in some parts kind of squashy and sticking to the snowshoes making them very heavy. Ever so often I would have to lift up the snowshoes and shake the snow off them for they would become quite heavy and awkward, but as bad as this was it did permit me a moment of rest and a chance to catch my breath.

Reaching the top of that hill, I came across several stacks of logs expertly cut and neatly placed alongside the road. Although they were covered with snow and one would not easily identify them as logs, I had seen them many times before in the summer months. How they came to be there is kind of a long story, but briefly, they had been cut by a couple of ex-convicts who had planned on selling them at a coal mine for props. But their brief enterprise was cut short by a Forest Ranger who reminded them that this was a National Forest and cutting of trees was not permitted. So here the logs lay and slowly rotting away, not doing anyone any good.

Murmuring Pines Cabin

I continued on my way, the time passing quickly, and soon I reached the turnoff to

Murmuring Pines Cabin. It lay down below to the left and its road descended downward staying parallel to the main road I was on. It wasn't more than two city blocks distance, and being downhill, I was at the cabin in no time. I had been here several times before, but always in summer. The snow was quite deep, being nearly as high as the door, so not being able to get in that way I had to enter through one of the windows. That was a little tricky since I was on snowshoe so I removed my pack and lowered it into the cabin and then removed the snowshoes and leaving them outside, I slid down through the opening.

I found the cabin in the same shape as I had last seen it. It had two large rooms; three tables whose surfaces porcupines had seriously gnawed; two beds; several windows were missing panes and the rest were boarded up. Years before it had contained more furniture, even a stove that is a very welcome piece of furniture to a traveler, but cabin pilfers had taken most everything. The roof being of tin was still intact and this assured a constant dry floor.

I placed my pack on one of the tables, untied the flap and removed the casserole and a package of crackers. There was a large square of tin on the floor where the stove had stood making a good place for a safe fire. Squirrels, or pack rats, had moved in a lot of sticks, so I used those for fuel and soon I had a fire going.

By removing several of the loose window boards, I created a flue to draw out the smoke. My can opener was on my knife, and it was rather difficult to operate and as I drew it across the can lid the blade broke and raked me across my left hand. I wasn't aware of the cut until I had finished opening the can with my sheath knife and placed the can on the fire. When I first saw my hand, I was quite startled. Not just at the sight of blood but at the amount of blood that had poured out over the floor. I reached outside and scooped up a handful of snow to scrub out the wound. The sudden cold seemed to help, for shortly the bleeding stopped and then I coated it with Merthiolate. I wrapped it with a torn piece of handkerchief and held it in place with a glove.

Letting the fire do its work on the casserole, I looked over the cabin. Since the cabin was a bit chilly and I being a little stiff from the exertion I had just put forth, moving around would help. A wall constructed out of lumber separated the two rooms. On this wall were numerous writings of those who had come before me and some, way before I was born. Like the caves of France where early man had left his impressions, here too was a similar reconstruction. *"Spent our honeymoon here. September 1914." "Found shelter here from a storm, Wendell & Rachel, 1938." "Spent two wonderful nights here, Bill & Clara, 1922."* And there was more and to join those of history, I too recorded my brief stay.

The spot of ground that the cabin rested upon was really a little island, as the owner, or early dweller, had excavated a ditch around the cabin and formed somewhat of a moat. It wasn't really that evident now because of the snow, but when I visited that place in the summer, it was quite noticeable. Perhaps it afforded one a better night's sleep feeling a little more secure from whatever might prowl around at night. Or maybe, one had read of a castle moat and after the evening meal, with nothing else to do, constructed the moat. I'm sure that it was much larger then than now as the ravages of time and weather had taken their toll and reduced its banks to just a step-over ditch.

Soon the aroma of the casserole diffused through the cabin and I removed the bubbling and steaming meal from the hot coals. In spite of it being hot, I ate hurriedly as I was rather upset over what had happened to my hand, but did not finish the meal as I couldn't locate the broken end of the can opener and thought perhaps it might be somewhere inside the casserole. And I didn't need something like that to get lodged in my throat so far away from any help.

I took out a cigar and lit it with and ember from the fire. I sat there and thought of the long trip still before me and already my shoulders were sore and my legs were beginning to tire form lifting the snow-coated snowshoes over the soft crust. I even contemplated spending the night here and let this be my journey's end. I could find a way to close off the other room, seal the missing windowpanes, and find enough wood to be cozy and do my writing. But, I had not brought along a sleeping bag because the Timberline Cabin had several old Army coats and I was planning on using those for cover. So, I decided to continue on much to my later dismay.

Back to the Road

I finished the smoke, spread an ample amount of snow on the fire remains, picked up my pack, buckled on my snowshoes and I was off to finish my trek to Timberline Cabin. I went directly up the hill through the trees to the road rather than retracing my steps, and that was really a challenge as the snow was deep and soft, and snow was falling off of the trees in large clumps and since they were wet and heavy, when they hit me their weight and speed would knock me nearly to the ground. Some of them sounded like an avalanche were taking place, and sometimes I would stop and look around to make sure one wasn't happening. After the first clump had shattered on and about my head, I paused and fastened the top button of my shirt and pulled down the flap on my hat, covering over the shirt collar, to prevent any of the snow from getting down my back. But despite the discomfort, taking this route was quicker than if I had retraced my steps. When I finally reached the road, I heaved a large sigh of relief and unbuttoned my shirt collar.

But even on the road, the going was tough. I continued on toward my destination. Once in a while the snow around me would give way in a wide circle like I was on a large pancake, sinking down perhaps a foot all around creating a ledge that I had to lift my snowshoes over. These were snow bridges I had come upon, and several had sunk so deep that in order for me to scale the ledge I had to remove one of the snowshoes, place it on the top of the ledge and climb out on top of it. And of course, this required my removing the pack and then having to put it back on. In spite of all this adversity, I stupidly continued on my journey.

Occasionally, when I stopped to rest, and if there was an opening between the trees, I would lift the binoculars to my eyes and study the rim of the mountain ridge on my left. Lee Minton had told me of a house built at the top of the rim many years ago by a miner and his daughter and in order to protect the gold mine from robbers, the house was placed over the shaft. I could see the house vaguely through the binoculars, but it was too far away to be distinct. Someday, I thought, I will climb up there and see it, in the summer of course, but the ascent is rugged and Lee informed me that it is a treacherous trip, and even in July, the nights are freezing cold. I scanned other parts of the rim and found enjoyment on being able to be almost up there. I always carried my binoculars. On a recent trip, I was looking through the binoculars and discovered a cabin. Had I been looking in that direction without those binoculars, the cabin would have appeared to be a large black boulder. So, they are definitely and asset on any trip.

The Old Saw Mill

After looking and resting a little bit, I shuffled my snowshoes onward toward timberline. I was climbing steadily and because of the altitude, the snow was becoming deeper. Then, just across the creek about fifty yards to my left, this huge house appeared. I had visited it several times during the summer, and Lee had told me then that it was a boarding house for the sawmill workers that at one time produced all the lumber for the many mining buildings on Democrat Mountain. Perhaps this is where the lumber came from that was used to build the Murmuring Pines cabin, the one I had just been to a little while ago. A porch ran the length of the front topped off with lots of Ginger Bread trimmings and the balusters and railings were all fancy cut pieces. There was a stream running along the West side of the house, a tributary to Bard Creek, now frozen and covered over with snow, that Lee Minton had told me, "follow that stream and it will take you right to the cabin on the rim." I paused for a moment reflecting on the entire goings on that could have taken place on that porch so many years ago. The conversations, the tobacco smoke, and the tobacco chewing, the smells from the kitchen, and whatever noises they might have made. Maybe someone had a fiddle, or guitar, maybe a harmonica that would soothe the soul and allow someone to rest after a grueling day of converting logs to lumber. Maybe horses whinnied in the back, or a donkey or burro braying for their oats.

I broke my melancholy and continued on the road. Shortly thereafter, the road ended turning into a foot path and Lee had told me that the road petered out about six miles from his cabin below, so I guessed from this that I had just about two more miles to go. The path was easily discernible in summer, but now, I just made my way where there was an opening in the dense forest. The trees were grouped so close together and the many small streams meandering around and about had cut deep crevices that forced me to search for the easiest place to cross over them. I could not maintain a straight line of traveling which made my trek longer and was using up precious daylight time. These streams and rivulets were the headwaters of Bard Creek. Some of the snow on the streams in the sun had melted away and exposed the rocky bottoms and wrestling my snowshoes across them wasn't easy to say the least. When I stepped on a rock, I had to make sure I put my weight on the middle of the snowshoe for the frame might splinter or rip out the leather bindings. Without those snowshoes, I could never make it back. Some of the rocks were under the water and the water would flow over the top of my boots soaking my socks. It was a most unpleasant sensation.

Continuing on and gaining altitude, the snow began changing its consistency from a slushy surface to that of powder, which caused me to sink deeper, but it didn't adhere to the webbing as the slush did. At least I didn't have to shake the slush off ever so often now, but since I sank down deeper, I had to lift the snowshoes higher. So, I traded one inconvenience for another.

I continued on, and was out of the stream area and had laboriously shuffled along for about a mile when I came to a clearing. My boots were wet through and through by now from having to fjord those streams, and I could feel the water squishing between my toes in the spongy socks. I paused for breath and while resting I looked at my watch. It was three o'clock. I was becoming concerned, as it would be nightfall in about two and a half hours, and I didn't know if I could find the cabin in the dark. And too, Lee had told me that he couldn't recall how much firewood was in the cabin, so I might have to dig some wood out of the snow, and it would be easier to do this digging by daylight. I wanted to go on, but I had to rest, as

I had covered around seven miles on heavy snowshoes and I was tired, also I wanted to drain the water out of my boots. I removed my pack and rifle and placed them on the snow, but when I unbuckled the snowshoes and stepped off of them, I went past my waist into the deep snow. I felt like being in quicksand. I struggled to get up but it was futile as the snow just gave way around me. I was panicked and then I grabbed hold of the snowshoes and placed them side-by-side and climbed out upon them like you would climb out of the water into a boat. I realized more than ever how vital it was to have those snowshoes. The snowshoes were my boat and I was afloat on a lake of snow. Regaining my composure, I carefully spread my parka out under me and removed the water-soaked boots and drained the water out of them. I undid my pack and got out a dry pair of socks and slipping of the wet ones, I placed the dry ones on my feet and I immediately felt the warmth they offered. I put the boots back on, and then not knowing just what to do with the wet socks, I wove them in and out of the snowshoe webbing not wanting to put them in the pack and get everything all wet.

I was hungry too, so I got out some chipped beef, crackers, and of course, some chocolate. I washed it all down with snow, and then lit a cigar, and as I smoked I pondered everything. Looking at my watch I saw that I had been sitting there for a half an hour. Too long I thought.

A Bull from the Brush

The foot of Bard Peak was not too far from this clearing, and the cabin was up its slope a little way. With that encouraging thought, I gathered up all my stuff and started shuffling out across the clearing. I had to go down through the clearing and then up again alongside a large stand of Buck Brush, and it was there in the brush that a noise startled me. A loud snort and sharp reports of breaking branches echoed up through the still canyon. Then I saw him. The largest bull elk I had ever laid eyes on. He broke free of the brush and pounced out into the clearing not over 100

COLLECTION OF TRUE STORIES: A NEAR DEATH EXPERIENCE

yards away. He stopped and faced me. Although he was belly deep in the snow, his head was held high and sported an antler spread that would have dwarfed any sportsman's collection. The cool mountain air vaporized his hurried breath streaming from his nostrils. His head nodded up and down as his hoofs churned the snow and tossed it about. My flesh tingled and a chill crept over me. *I spooked his cows in the brush,* I surmised, *and now he's mad as hell.* I brought the lever down on the 30-30 and I heard the familiar click as a round slid into the chamber and the hammer was cocked. I knew the caliber was too small for such a huge beast, but hopefully the sound might deter him. I had no choice. It was the only defense I had.

He stared at me - and I back at him. Being on snowshoes, I could not move fast and here in an open field, there was nothing to move too, so I stood still. I was in his territory, and he was in command. I was frightened silly and hoped that I didn't freeze in my boots and couldn't react if he decided to come at me.

He continued tossing his head and pawing at the snow. Then he stopped his show, bellowed a long eerie sound that chilled me even more. He reared back and gave a long and loud bugle, lowered his head and then came charging at me at a mad pace. His huge antlers, lowered, just barely skimming the snow, were coming at me fast. I don't know how I did it, but I got off three rounds over his head as rapidly as I could and the roar of those shots caused him to swerve aside and change his attitude of a full charge. As he galloped past me, the snow he kicked up flew into my face and down into my open shirt. I turned quickly, as best I could, to cover my rear in case he came again. He was gone. His tracks followed my snowshoe trail and disappeared over the rise. Much to my surprise I was still standing, appreciating that I had brought the rifle with me, even though it was of a small caliber. Its noise had done the trick. No rear attack, no dead elk, no blood, nothing. Just silent tracks.

I stared at the place where his tracks disappeared for a little while making sure he didn't decide to return and catch me off guard.

I reloaded the carbine and nervously proceeded on, but as I continued, I found myself looking back over my shoulder. I have never traveled with a bullet in the chamber of the carbine, for safety reasons, but after that experience I deemed it necessary to do so.

Another Close Call

The forest became denser and the snow powdery. The trail lead upward constantly and I found my legs becoming more tired causing my strides to shorten and not able to cover as much ground as before.

Rounding a large boulder, I was startled again, this time by a huge eagle and he was just as startled as I was. He winged his way upward in my direction from a freshly killed rabbit. He was very defiant and probably thought I was interested in his meal, but having had enough excitement for one day, I gave him and the rabbit a wide berth. I seemed to be immune to his threat probably, because of the size of the threat I had just experienced.

The Base of Bard Peak

Familiar landmarks began to appear and the trail took on a steeper ascent. I knew that I was at the base of Bard Peak reassuring me that the cabin wasn't too much further. But it lay uphill a way, and it was steep, and the snow was soft. I was tired and decided to rest just a bit and study just where to begin the ascent. I chose a spot that didn't seem as steep as the other side and I thought I could switch back and forth traversing the slope, but to no avail. I couldn't get started upward, for when I took a step with my left snowshoe it would sink down and when I attempted a step with the right snowshoe, the left one would slide backwards, and so it went. And too, I didn't have the strength to wage such a battle.

I then realized I was not going to make it up the final leg of the journey to the cabin. I looked at my watch. It was five o'clock. The sun had disappeared behind Bard Peak causing the temperature to drop rapidly and I could feel the chill standing here at the base of the rise. My shoulders were sore from the weight of the pack, and my wet feet were now beginning to feel the pangs of the cold. I couldn't spend the night here just below timberline. I had no sleeping bag or blankets, and firewood was buried under four or five feet of snow. And where could I find a clearing to erect a lean-to or other shelter that would afford me protection from the oncoming sub-zero temperature. Yes, it was quite clear, regardless of physical fatigue, I must return. For here I was, alone, miles from nowhere at the base of timber line, in deep snow, boots full of water, no sleeping bag, unable to go any farther, and the freezing temperature of the night was fast approaching.

I Must Turn Back

My choice of what to do was more evident than I wanted to admit, but I must turn back, and forsake my trip to the Timberline Cabin. I had no other choice. After all, that I had gone through, and the cabin was not more than four or five hundred yards, but it was impossible to reach it. A thought chilled me. *I could die here if I don't do this right.* I have to go back. At least the return back is all downhill and the trail is packed down and should be easy to follow even in the dark. Strangely enough, I found comfort in that thought and decided to return, not all the way, but to the Murmuring Pines Cabin. I wished now I had stayed there to start with, but I hadn't. The cabin had plenty of firewood

COLLECTION OF TRUE STORIES: A NEAR DEATH EXPERIENCE

available, and I could take the tables and form a little room around the fire. It wouldn't be the best, but I'd be inside and a fire would keep off the freezing night. I could dry out my feet, have some instant coffee, a fine cigar, and just let the night pass away. I was encouraged now, and found a revival of renewed strength. I knew I could make it that far, but not confident that I could make it all the way back to Lee Minton's cabin as tired as I was.

I made a wide circle and started retracing my snowshoe trail, but with too much vigor, for one of the snowshoe tips crossed over the other one that I was lifting up and I went head first into four feet of snow. The leather harnesses on the snowshoes were water soaked and stretched

172

out of shape allowing the snowshoes to wobble and hard to control. The weakened and tired condition of my leg muscles was unable to counteract such a fall. I cleared away enough snow around me providing the necessary arm space to remove my heavy pack and to unbuckle the snowshoes. I lined the snowshoes up side by side, as I had learned to do, and climbed out on top of them. Supported by the snowshoes, I reached down and retrieved my pack and rifle. I placed them on the forward top of the snowshoes and, removing my gloves, I loosened the straps and readjusted the tension of the harness. My injured finger kept getting in the way, and I had two goals now. To adjust the harness as best I could and quit banging my sore finger. Both were feeble attempts, but I did manage, and when I finally buckled the snowshoes onto the boots, I could feel the difference. They were now tight and I hoped they would not stretch anymore. Wearily, I lifted the pack to my sore shoulders, picked up my rifle, and then in the dwindling light I saw the bull elk high up on the ridge looking down at me. Probably wondering what that poor clumsy human was doing. He turned then and disappeared on the other side. Several other shadowy figures followed close behind. His cows I guess, so he shouldn't present any problem.

Slowly and cautiously I started the retracing of my steps. The harness tightening had remedied the wobble in the snowshoes and as I walked and got the circulation going again in my legs, some of the tiredness left them and going downhill in a packed-down trail was a lot easier than going up and breaking trail. Also, I did not have to make any decisions as which way to go which was a relief to me and I was making good time.

I found myself entering the clearing where I had met "Mr. Elk" and dipping down through it and up again, I came to the spot where I had rested some two hours previous. Had I turned back here, I thought, it would have placed me back at the Murmuring Pines cabin by now. But I hadn't, so, no need to even think about it. On I trudged, for I wanted to get past the streams and reach the road before it got too dark. And presently I did. I reached the streams and having a trail to follow I got through them much easier than before, but I did pick up some more water in my boots. I reached the road shortly thereafter and stopped and removed my pack and crouched down, rather awkwardly on the snowshoes. I unbuckled the flap on the pack and felt down inside and moved my hand around until I located the flashlight and an apple. I placed the pack under my behind so I could sit down without having to remove the snowshoes, and then took a bite out of the apple. It was cold and the sweet flavor revitalized my strength and my spirits. I tested the flashlight and it cast a bright beam piercing the darkness with a confident air. I was thankful I had the notion of putting new batteries in it just a few days ago. I continued eating the apple and sitting there in the dark. The night air was becoming quite cold so finishing the apple, I put my parka on. It felt warm and comfortable and it made my pack lighter too, although the weight was still on me. But the shift of parka's weight did seem to help as I once again headed down the trail. The trail stood out rather well in the darkness. I only shinned the light when I was in doubt or wanted to recognize a landmark.

There must have been a herd of deer or elk using the road as there began to be other tracks appearing alongside my trail and sometimes in it. I wasn't concerned about this, but I should have been.

No Saw Mill and Too Many Tracks

The next landmark to watch for was the sawmill. It would be hard to locate in the dark, as it lay so far off to the right of the road and across the creek. I was sure I knew the twists and turns of the road well enough to locate it, and I felt that I needed to recognize it for Murmuring Pines cabin was just a short distance away from it.

I fell several more times as I couldn't see those sunken snow bridges and the ledges weren't discernible in the darkness. I had to repeat the arduous task each time of removing the snowshoes, placing them on the rim and climbing up onto them.

I kept trudging on through the darkness following my old trail and those of the deer or elk. Sometimes it was hard to differentiate their tracks from mine. But regardless of who's tracks, I kept going, and shinning the light occasionally into the darkness on the right side looking for a sign of the sawmill. I found none, and, except for the trail that went on and on, I felt like I was lost. I'm sure it was just ahead and that was my thought as I rounded each curve, but it seemed so elusive and I couldn't figure out why I hadn't come upon it. Then after a little bit farther, I noticed several mounds of snow off to my right. I stopped and stared. "No, it couldn't be!" I exclaimed aloud. "Those can't be the piles of logs?" I asked myself aloud. I left the trail and walked over to one of the piles and wiped off the layer of snow. Logs appeared in my light. I was happy and sad at the same time. I was happy that I had come this far, but sad that I had missed Murmuring Pines. I had not been able to find the sawmill in the darkness and since I was so concentrated on finding it, I had overlooked the trail I had made earlier coming up through the trees from Murmuring Pines. I should have been concentrating on that trail more so than the sawmill, but I hadn't. I hadn't noticed the trail leading off of the road and into the trees because of all the tracks the animals had made. I thought that I was following my old snowshoe tracks at that point, but I was following their tracks instead.

Well, I said to myself. *I'm not going back to Murmuring Pines. I'll continue on to Lee's cabin.* And so, I did. I shuffled on down the steep hill to the Bard Creek Mill without stopping and then on to the flats and finally I arrived at the Beaver Dam Cabin. With much exhaustive effort, I managed to reach the porch. I removed my pack and sat down on the inverted can that I had sat on what seemed like ages ago. I got another apple from my pack and proceeded to eat it. My eyes kept closing and then reopening. The apple fell from my hand as my head nodded. I was so warm, and my legs felt the rest they had needed for so long. I shinned the light on my watch. It was 8 o'clock. I had been on the snowshoes now for eleven hours. I had expended more physical output than I would have exerted in a month at the office. My head nodded again, and I began to feel so warm and I only wanted to sleep. I knew though not to fall asleep, exhausted as I was, and in this freezing temperature, I would surely die, but there was no resistance in me. I felt so warm and relaxed.

Suddenly, I was brought back to my senses by a loud report like that of a canon coming from just across the road. And then another blast burst out of the darkness bringing me quickly and fully alert and ready for whatever. Then several more smaller and softer sounds resounded after the first two, and then I realized what it was. The beavers on the pond across the road were slapping their tails on the water. They had saved my life. "Thank you, Beavers," I yelled to them.

I staggered to my feet, but my legs buckled from under me and I had to steady myself for a little bit against the cabin wall. After a few wobbly steps, up and down the porch, I believed I could go on. I buckled on the snowshoes and reached down and only picked up my carbine. The pack, I left it there, and without it I noticed a big difference in my stability and movement. It should have been left many miles up the road.

Despite this lightweight advantage, my trip to Lee's cabin was not without its spills. My legs, being so tired and sore were unable to hold me up when I slipped or tripped. These spills, however, weren't as bad as the ones higher up the road as the snow here wasn't as deep, and minus the pack, I didn't have as difficult a time righting myself.

The snowshoes crunched on through the snow, and I could hear the familiar sound the tail ends made as they scraped across the crust reminding me with each sound I was still moving forward.

When I came down the last hill and rounded the turn to Lee's cabin, I was again dismayed, for there was no light shining from the front window. Maybe he had decided to join his wife, Helen, at their lower cabin, which lay three miles further down the road. I couldn't walk that distance. Even the small climb up to his front door was going to be laborious. By this time, his two dogs were raising a howl, as they always do when someone approaches.

I managed the small climb and was rounding the cabin to the door when a flashlight beam pierced the night. It was Lee and I was most thankful that he was home. He later told me that no lights were on as he had retired unusually early that evening.

He had to help me unbuckle the snowshoes and half carried me into the kitchen where he immediately got the wood stove to burning. I removed my boots and placed my feet, with the wet socks on, into the oven. It was nine o'clock. For twelve hours, I had battled my way up and back from timberline.

It wasn't long before the teakettle water was boiling and Lee placed a hot cup of coffee in my hand. It burned all the way down, but it was a pleasant burn.

The End

"The Wingless Bat"; "The Dawn of Time"; "Turan" the panther, and "Three Boys in the Jungle," to name a few. Dan has drawn inspiration for writing from his imagination and personal experiences. Since writing his first novel as a young teen, Dan has built a legacy of short stories and mysteries including his children's book; the many Adventures of Croaker the Frog. Dan's stories engage and surprise the reader with unexpected twist endings keeping the audience curious to the very end. This book is a must read.

Do you have a comment, question or story
that you would like to share with Dan Fields?
Send to: danfieldsenterprise@gmail.com

Made in the USA
Columbia, SC
09 August 2018